JOB HUNTING FOR PHYSICIANS

TIPS FOR RESIDENTS, FELLOWS, AND OTHER JOB SEEKERS

LAURIE MORGAN, MBA

MANAGEMENT RX

ISBN (paperback, 6x9): 978-1-970044-21-8

CONTENTS

PART FOUR: INTERVIEWING AND DECISION MAKING

INTRODUCTION

For the past dozen-plus years, I've worked as a practice management consultant, author, and freelance writer on the business side of medicine. Through these roles, I've had the opportunity to recruit physicians on behalf of practice clients; help practices welcome and integrate new hires into their practices; diagnose and work through conflicts in practice businesses; and interview dozens of physicians to gain their perspectives on the job-hunting process.

Some of what I've learned is reflected in Chapters 4 through 13, most of which were originally published as features (in shorter form) in *PracticeLink* magazine. In those stories, you'll hear quotes from physicians who've already progressed to different stages of their careers in a wide variety of settings. Some of their helpful comments were abridged or edited out (when necessary for length) when originally published in the magazine; here, you'll get them in full.

These fellow physicians shared their views to help you make better, clearer decisions and avoid the mistakes that they or their colleagues have made. They hope that what they've learned will make your first steps on the physician career path a bit smoother.

At the start of this book, you'll find several chapters that distill my own perspective on job hunting. I've chosen to spotlight mistakes I hope you'll avoid, based on what I've learned as a consultant and as someone who's recruited physicians (and who was an employee in various businesses for many years, too). I'm coming at it from the perspective of a businessperson who's worked with physicians, which I hope enables me to give you a few fresh ideas.

Businesspeople begin learning about job hunting while still finishing their undergraduate degrees. The rules (written and unwritten) and best practices are passed down to entire classes of undergrads at one time. As we all nervously figure things out, we learn with the help of campus career centers and books, and by simply talking to one another. Once it starts, the learning about job hunting and career planning in business never really stops. As businesspeople proceed through their careers—commonly changing jobs every few years—the important customs of the job market become second nature.

The principles of the job-hunting process and the etiquette involved are so established and well known in the business world, I hope I can be forgiven for initially assuming you already knew them, too. Managing your career is simply a thing you do when you work in business (especially for people like me who went on to pursue an MBA). It's more or less part of your job.

When I began working with medical practices in 2010, though, it dawned on me quickly that this bit of acculturation doesn't happen for everyone in their twenties—especially not physicians. You're far too busy burning the candle at both ends in your training to care about planning for something that's still many years away. (And I bet that many of you simply think "I just want to take care of patients," anyway.)

To understand what the job search looks like to a resident or fellow leaving training, I had to put myself back in the shoes of my wet-behind-the-ears self, approaching the job search with no experience to guide me, desperate to sell myself, and hoping I'd somehow land a gig that would set me on the right path forward.

Well... no. That's not exactly right. Because you, of course, are older and much wiser than a recent college grad. That will help you. Much more important: You're not really "just starting out." Unlike the typical newbie in business, you already have exceedingly rare and valuable skills to offer patients and a prospective employer. You just need to figure out how to put those skills to work in the place that's right for *you*.

I hope you've internalized that last important fact, because part of your challenge will be balancing your need and desire to sell yourself with the opportunity to be more self-focused than you probably have been in years. Not framing the job search as a mix of selling *and* buying is one of the more common missteps I've seen beginning physicians make.

Once you know you should do this (and why), being too focused on employers' hiring decisions and too little on your career priorities becomes an avoidable mistake. Learning to avoid it means reducing the risk that you'll miss out on the job that's just right for you.

———

Where to start in this book

In PART ONE (Chapters 1 through 3), I discuss some of the avoidable job-search mistakes I've known physicians to make. I think it's a natural place to start thinking about how to approach your job search.

Of course, it's not essential to read the chapters in order. If you prefer to begin with some nuts and bolts, another good place to start is with the timeline discussion in Chapter 4 and Chapter 5, followed by CV prep in Chapter 6.

PART ONE: MISTAKES TO LEARN FROM

CHAPTER 1: MISTAKES JOB-HUNTING PHYSICIANS MAKE —AND HOW TO AVOID THEM

RESEARCH AND TARGETING, PRESENTATION, AND INTERVIEWING MISTAKES

By popular estimates, as many as half of graduating physicians wind up dissatisfied with their first jobs, leaving for new opportunities within the first few years.

This pattern isn't just an inconvenience for those unlucky physicians (or the organizations that hire them). Switching jobs can be quite costly for a physician, especially when they're just starting out. A key reason is that first-job switches often mean a change of location, whether because the physician found they'd chosen a part of the country they didn't like or because a non-compete agreement in their employment contract forced them to leave the market.

Building a practice (and all the referral relationships that keep it growing) takes time. Since physician compensation is usually at least partially dependent on productivity, when a doctor must start over at building a patient base, their income is likely affected. Pulling up stakes for a new hometown also almost surely comes at a cost, even if a relocation allowance is secured. This is especially true for physicians with families or those whose spouses or life partners will also need to find new employment.

There's also the toll on mental health. Moving and job changing are two of life's most stressful events. Starting over after realizing a first job was a poor fit means reigniting both of these stressors when you've just started to rebound from them.

The worst part? Many physicians who find they made a regrettable job choice might have been able to avoid that costly false start.

That's exactly what this chapter (and this book) are all about: helping physicians like you improve your chances of bypassing the jobs that won't fit your personality and goals—and homing in on the ones that line up best.

Here, and in the next chapter, are my favorite tips to easily avoid common mistakes and instead take proactive steps for a more successful, less stressful job search.

Research and Targeting Mistakes

Research mistake #1: Not thinking through your wants and needs

I've already mentioned that far too many physicians find themselves dissatisfied with their first jobs, bearing the disappointment and cost of starting the job search all over again.

This may not be preventable for every physician in their first job. Some jobs may need to be experienced before the characteristics that make them unsuitable for a particular person become apparent. But many unsuccessful job choices surely *are* avoidable.

One reason for suboptimal choices stems from physicians' prior experiences, especially in training.

From getting into med school to pursuing residencies and fellowships, physicians become accustomed to selling themselves. As undergrads and med students, future physicians hope to be chosen. To a large extent, you're at the mercy of the choosers. It's a repetitive process of putting your best foot forward and hoping you wind up with what you want.

But once you've made it through the ridiculously competitive string of hurdles that is physician training, the balance of power shifts—and not all newly minted physicians fully grasp how much.

For the rest of your career, barring an unusual catastrophe, you're likely to be in very high demand. Where you want to go, the kind of medicine you want to practice, who you want to work with, and what kind of culture you want to immerse yourself in—these are all questions you should consider before you embark on your job search.

Do you know where you'd like to live for the foreseeable future—and why? If you're thinking of moving someplace temporarily (or staying where you've been training temporarily), have you sketched out a plan for what comes next?

Do you dream of owning a practice one day? (Or do you hope you'll never have to own your own practice?)

Are you willing to give up some schedule flexibility to earn more money? (Or vice versa?)

Do you dream of participating in research? Does being on the cutting edge of medicine matter to you? (And is that more, or less, important than how much you'll earn?)

Do you have a social mission you hope to fulfill with your work? (Could that ambition be satisfied by spending a few years in an under-served area, or by practicing overseas? Or do envision working long-term in a clinic in a low-income area?)

Are you interested in concierge medicine? Value-based care? Academic medicine? Non-clinical work?

Do you need variety? Have you thought about how you'll find that in your physician career?

These questions are probably just the tip of the iceberg! But I hope you get the idea—and let yourself think about all that *you* want from your job.

Of course, you won't necessarily get everything you want—at least not at first. But you can set your course to do so. And hopefully, with thoughtful planning, you'll avoid choosing something that's not a step in the right direction for you.

If all of this sounds oddly self-centered to you, here's another reason to think long and hard about what you want: Employers want you to!

At least the smart ones do. Why? Because physician turnover is even more costly for them than it is for you.

Recruiting and hiring a physician is a significant investment. When a doctor leaves a first job within a couple of years, odds are that physician hasn't reached profitable productivity or been productive for long enough for the employer to recoup their costs.

Employers are also enormously concerned about burnout and morale. The last thing they want is for their employed doctors to feel they don't fit in!

So now's the time for you to be a little more self-focused. Don't feel the least bit guilty about it. Remind yourself that prospective employers want you to be choosy. In fact, if you seem too eager to please or too ready to say yes to everything, that can even be a red flag in the interview process.

Research mistake #2: Relying too heavily on physician job boards and headhunters

When you're working in business, there's a basic job-search lesson you learn early on: the best job for you might not be advertised. While discussed less in medicine, it's true in physician hiring, too.

Contingency and retained recruiters are expensive (they typically charge twenty to thirty percent of first year physician pay). That cost is significant enough that some organizations only use external recruiters when they've found a job "impossible" to fill. (This alone ought to give you some pause, or at least raise some questions you should be sure to ask.)

Hiring organizations also note with frustration that commission-based recruiters are often so focused on placing as many physicians as possible, they're not as concerned about finding the right fit as they ideally would be. (That's not good news for either candidates or employers.)

Job-board advertising is also expensive. A single ad can cost thousands of dollars per board, and there are loads of boards out there: big sites like PracticeLink that serve all physicians; boards linked to key medical journals (e.g., *JAMA* and *NEJM*); specialty society and association job boards; general job sites like Indeed; etc., etc., etc. It's a big investment to blanket these resources.

These costs are why most jobs you see that are either repped by external recruiters or posted all over physician job databases are with major hospitals and large health systems.

Independent groups and hospitals and smaller health systems may only be able to choose one or two places to post. They may also try to save money by choosing lower visibility ad packages or shorter ad durations. If you don't go to that particular board during the window they're advertising—or scan too quickly—you can miss that smaller, less prominent posting.

Another reason a great job might be "invisible": Some prospective employers, especially independent practices, might not be actively *looking* to add a physician, but still able to hire opportunistically if contacted by a great candidate. (Or, as I've seen so often in my consulting work, they've been absolutely desperate to bring on a new doctor but being short a physician has left them too busy to take the steps to do it!)

So how do you find these unpublished jobs?

In business, everyone learns that most of the best jobs are found through networking. You expand your network by meeting different people in your target industry and asking for help (usually not by pitching them—just by making connections). Eventually, if all goes according to plan, after persistent rounds of handshaking and coffee-dating, you'll meet someone who knows someone who needs someone just like you.

As a busy resident or fellow, you might find the idea of taking dozens of coffee meetings to build your network daunting (or even completely unrealistic, particularly if you hope to land a job in a different region). But the good news is that digging up hidden physician job opportunities doesn't have to follow this exact pattern.

Even in business, networking, like so many other things, has been transformed by the internet. The pandemic has only reinforced the move to electronic and virtual forms of networking.

Connections can be made on social media like LinkedIn and Facebook (e.g., through groups organized by specialty). These tools are fantastic for *maintaining* connections you've made in the past, too —medical school friends and even people you knew in college (groups and mailing lists are great for this purpose). Remember that your network is already wider and deeper than you might think.

Networking works in job hunting because when you ask nicely and considerately, people almost always want to help. The considerate part is that you're not asking anyone to "give you a job." You're looking for information and advice and maybe a push in the right direction. If a contact who's connected to you in some fashion (say, a friend of a friend, or a member of the same online group) knows someone who's been hoping to hire a physician in your specialty, why wouldn't they tell you about that situation? It's possible they'd be helping two people with one small favor.

Here's something else: it's also OK to reach out cold. Feel free to contact the local medical association in the local area you hope to work in. Even if they don't have their own job board, the director of the association will likely know if any member practices in your specialty are on the hunt for a physician. Odds are that even if not, that person will be glad to have met you (especially since you're contemplating a move to their area) and may even have a suggestion for a practice you might contact. (And there you are... painlessly networking.)

Some medical associations and specialty societies have affiliated administrator and manager groups. Don't overlook them in your outreach. If your research turns up a practice that seems a perfect fit for you, contact the administrator of that group. Any administrator charged with the tough task of finding physician candidates will likely be grateful to hear from you. Just be sure your CV comes with a cover letter that's well-crafted and targeted, so that the administrator doesn't have to guess at why you're getting in touch with them specifically.

Starting with the administrator can be a route to getting a quick answer, since the manager of a group is often in charge of all recruiting. But this doesn't mean you shouldn't reach out to physicians as well—especially if you've made a mutual connection through networking. Again, just be sure you've prepared well and can concisely explain (in your cover letter, CV, and/or by phone) why you've reached out to the physician and their practice in particular.

Research mistake #3: Starting too late

While the pull of procrastination may be strong, you'll feel more relaxed and in control of the job search if you start early. Networking and research, wrangling administrative details, and selecting expert help will all be much easier with less time pressure.

Since you just finished reading Mistake #2, you've probably already figured out that networking, even just re-establishing old connections, takes time. So does research, especially when considering a move to a different part of the country. Job hunting will seem less daunting if you start slowly and take it bit by bit. You'll also do a more thorough job of it.

"Networking" and "research" can just mean talking with residents and fellows who are a year or two ahead of you. Draft behind them and pick up tidbits they're learning about different settings and organizational cultures. It's a low-stress way to learn. Don't let the idea that it's "too early" stop you from casually gathering information about job options and the search process.

When those colleagues complete training and move on to jobs, they can provide invaluable feedback about what worked out well and what they wish they'd done differently. Once employed, they'll meet many other physicians and discover organizations they never crossed paths with during their job search.

For example, if you've decided to look for a setting with a specific characteristic—say, a hospital that's been a leader on new payment models or a group that's certified as a PCMH—it may not be as straightforward as searching online. Sometimes the details you're after aren't publicized. Tips and leads from colleagues ahead of you can be especially helpful in this situation. (So don't lose touch with them.)

Medical school and even college friends can be helpful to your research, too. Friends can give you insight into what it's like to live in a city you're considering, and even non-physicians can comment on patient experiences with different local practices.

Besides relaxed and thorough research and networking, starting earlier gives you time to organize details that can be a pain to deal with under a deadline. When you're ready to evaluate offers and make a decision, you and your future employer will both be glad you're well-prepared.

For example, credentialing and licensing take (costly) time. But it's possible to get a jump on these key administrative tasks early in your last year of training (if not before).

In case it's still new to you, a simplified explanation: credentialing is the process by which commercial and government payers confirm your qualifications prior to adding you to their networks. Unsurprisingly, payers want lots of detailed information from many sources. (Hospitals similarly want to verify your credentials and your scope of practice before granting privileges.)

Until your credentialing is complete, your employer won't be able to bill health plans for your services. Consequently, credentialing new hires as quickly as possible is always an urgent priority for employers!

What's more, insurance companies receive a deluge of credentialing applications from new graduates in the summer, so processing times swell. (Even during less busy seasons, the process will take *months*.) If you're well-prepared, you'll enable your employer to submit your credentials to payers faster, improving the chances of your paperwork being first in line. If that leads to a faster credentialing response, you can start billing insurance faster, too.

You won't be able to complete the credentialing process on your own, nor should you expect to. Employers have credentialing specialists to manage submissions for their contracted plans (and all the labor-intensive back-and-forth with payers). But before they can begin, the next most time-consuming part of credentialing—the legwork of gathering your documentation—falls to you. You can get a jump on this while still in residency, starting with setting up your identity on CAQH (caqh.org), the credentialing information exchange used by most payers and hospitals.

Going through the CAQH process may also spotlight the specifics that employers, hospitals, and payers are interested in when hiring in your specialty. Throughout the interview process, it will save time for you and employers if you're up front about the credentials you have (or will have when you complete training). Employers need to know you've met or are on track to meet their specific requirements for your scope of practice.

Licensing in the state where you plan to practice is another task you can usually get a jump on. The time required varies widely by state, but once you know where you're going, you can start the process (for example, learning what documentation is required and in what formats). State licensing may also be a prerequisite for board certification—which in turn may be required by your employer.

As with everything else credential-related, the sooner you accomplish these things, the sooner you'll be ready to go to work for your new employer. Keeping close track of the timing and required order of these tasks will help you provide your new employer with reliable information about your readiness to practice.

Another bottleneck you can prevent before you even receive an offer: finding an attorney and/or compensation consultant to help you negotiate.

Prospective employers are unlikely to be concerned that you want legal review of your physician contract or if you're working through the compensation plan with the help of a consultant. If that process takes weeks because you haven't yet lined up your expert help, though, that could turn into a burden for your future employer.

Recommendations for attorneys and compensation experts are another great reason to stay in touch with all the physicians you befriend during training. Finding someone you can trust to help with legal matters is essential, and you don't want to do it under time pressure if you can avoid it.

More nuts and bolts of your job search timeline, plus some reasons why you should start earlier than others might recommend, are discussed in Chapter 4.

Presentation Mistakes

Presentation mistake #1: Not including a (custom) cover letter

Online job boards make it so easy to click-and-shoot a CV to an in-house recruiter that it may not seem worth the effort to add a cover letter.

Some people may even tell you that "nobody reads cover letters, anyway."

Don't believe them—especially when applying for a job you're particularly interested in.

Employers are increasingly sensitive to physician turnover. Since lack of knowledge about what a job or a location is like increases the risk of physician dissatisfaction, employers want to know you've done your homework. Your cover letters are your chance to show that you have. Use them to let employers know that you're interested in *their* opportunity, not just *an* opportunity.

If you still doubt that a cover letter's important, would you be surprised to know that I've worked with clients who won't even consider a CV that arrives without one?

It doesn't take long to write a cover letter, and it can make all the difference. Write that custom cover letter!

For more on why and how to craft a cover letter, see Chapter 7.

Presentation mistake #2: Not tailoring your CV

In business, customizing a resume (say, for a particular industry or type of role) is common. For example, businesspeople often put an objective or summary at the top of the page, hoping to spotlight their interest in a particular field. Under each position listed, they'll tailor the accomplishments to those most relevant to the job they're seeking.

Should physicians imitate this custom?

Adding a general objective won't help much (e.g., "provide patient-centered care in a children's hospital setting"). But some CV customizations can make a difference and sell the fact that you've done your research, such as when you're aiming for a very specific type of role or setting.

Some examples: If you're looking for a non-clinical job; have a special interest in research an employer engages in; or hope to work in an environment with a particular care-team approach or compensation model, these could all be worth mentioning at the top when you apply. This signals from the first interaction your genuine interest in the employer's mission or strategy. Aside from creating a custom objective, you should also be sure your CV promotes any experiences you have (or publications) that relate directly to the objective.

Of course, these CV customizations would be used just for an application to a relevant employer. It's perfectly normal to have more than one version of your CV for these purposes.

Customizing around a specific objective may not be the most fundamental type of tailoring you should think about, though. You should also consider whether and how you should pare down your CV. A CV including every one of your publications is essential for an academic application, even if the document runs ten pages; for a rural hospital or private group, on the other hand, it might suggest your expectations are mismatched to the position.

More ideas on CV tailoring and editing are discussed in Chapter 6.

Presentation mistake #3: Bungling document basics

Whatever environment you're aiming for, you'll want to avoid common CV mistakes that make it harder for recruiters and hiring physicians to understand or appreciate your background.

For example, you may have gotten into the habit of listing your experiences chronologically, but the expected format for a CV is *reverse* chronological order. This allows the reader to see your most recent accomplishments first. Important credentials (such as your board and licensing status) should be easy to find. And if you're a resident or fellow, your year and academic credentials should also typically be at the top of the first page.

Another practical error that's easy to avoid: don't forget to include your name, cell (text) number, city and state, and email at the top of the first page. Remember that even though you may prefer texting, the person reading your CV may be accustomed to contacting candidates by email. Include all the channels so that the employer can reach you by their preferred method. Including your city and state makes it easier for a recruiter to know your time zone for scheduling.

Saving your CV as a PDF ensures that what you see on screen is what the recipient will see. PDF makes printing easy and reliable, too. And because CVs are often printed and distributed, subsequent pages should all have your name and a way to contact you (along with page number), so that the reader can still reach you if part of your CV is misplaced.

And above all, make sure you've carefully proofread both your CV and cover letter. Ideally, have someone else take a look. (You could trade off with a friend, for example, if you're both good at proofreading and grammar.) Make sure you're using parallel grammatical structure for your bullets, and that your formatting is consistent throughout the document, too.

Triple-check that you've addressed your cover letter to the right person and organization. (Cut-and-paste can create these embarrassing problems—yet another reason to customize cover letters.)

And if you're unfamiliar with how to format your CV—i.e., with the basics of headings, bullets, font choices, etc.—look for a template online.

See Chapter 6 for more on crafting your perfect CV.

Presentation mistake #4: Not tidying social media

As of this writing, if you're a resident or fellow, it's possible you've had social media accounts since you were in middle school. It's also possible that some of the information contained on those pages might be less than helpful to your job search.

Did you engage in activities as a youngster (or college student?) that don't reflect who you are now, as a physician? Or that you advise patients against?

It might be a good idea to scrub your accounts of views that don't reflect your true self, or that could be misunderstood or misconstrued. (Or at least to review your online identities to be sure.)

And whether or not you decide to do any editing, check your privacy settings. It may be impossible to completely lock down social profiles, but you can make it less likely that hiring managers will stumble onto anything too personal. (This is also a good idea because you're about to start building a practice and will want to keep your personal life separate from your professional, public one.)

While your *personal* social media might benefit from some culling, you might want to add to your *professional* social media presence.

For example, you likely have profiles already on the big physician reviews and ratings sites (e.g., Healthgrades), because they're automatically established. But taking the time to claim your profile, spiff it up (e.g., with a professional photo), and correct any errors will give you a jump on marketing your new practice. And if you don't have a LinkedIn profile, the start of a job search is a good time to add one.

Presentation mistake #5: Insufficiently preparing for virtual interviews

COVID has likely changed job hunting forever. Most job searches will start with at least one interview over Zoom (or a similar platform), especially if you're targeting jobs outside your current location.

In the early days of virtual interviewing, suboptimal set-ups were forgivable. Now that virtual interviewing is commonplace, though, you'll do yourself a disservice if you don't look your relaxed best online.

Lighting makes a big difference, and lights designed for video chat are very inexpensive. Experiment with what works best. (One tip a photographer taught me: Bouncing the light off a wall behind the camera, rather than aiming it at your face, creates a softer, more flattering light.)

Be sure to figure out how best to set up your camera so that you can be relaxed during a lengthy conversation. Find a spot that's easy to keep neat so that you don't have to rush around cleaning before each interview. If an employer wants to use a platform you don't normally use, you may not be able to set up a custom or blurred background before your call.

Interviewing Mistakes

Interviewing mistake #1: One-sided interviewing

Too many job seekers don't realize how important it is to show up to their interviews prepared not just to answer questions, but to ask them.

Your questions are the clearest way to show the interviewer that you're genuinely informed about and interested in their organization.

It's not just about stroking their egos. Even the largest employers can only hire so many physicians. For those few critical roles, they don't want to hire based on credentials and clinical skills alone. They're hoping for a match that will last. They want to hire physicians who'll stay long enough to earn back their hiring costs, and they want their teams to gel and reinforce the culture they've fostered. Your sincere interest is one of the best ways they have to confirm you'll be a good fit.

Employers also know that if you've done research and ask intelligent questions, you're more likely to be ready to accept an offer. That saves them from wasting valuable time courting candidates whose interest is fleeting.

As important as it is to ask questions (and make sure you get the answers you need), though, there are a few pitfalls to be aware of.

First, be conscious of timing. It's probably not a good idea to ask about compensation very early in the process; that can come across a bit like proposing marriage on the first date, or as if you're focused on pay above all other factors, both of which can be a turnoff.

And beware of a related stumbling block: Be sure you're posing your question to the right person.

For example, the in-house recruiter may not be the best person to ask about culture in a clinic or details of the schedule, or about how staff and physicians interact. But that recruiter will likely be precisely the right person to connect you with people with the answers: your would-be boss, the group administrator, or fellow physicians. (Again, you'll get your most detailed feedback, and the chance to see for yourself, if you ask when the time is right, such as when you've been invited to visit.)

And if you find you didn't get a complete answer to a question or the answer just doesn't make sense, that could be a sign you should ask someone else for more detail.

With compensation, for example, it may be less awkward to start with the recruiter when you're confused, need to verify details, or are broaching the subject for the first time. But if you're digging into a productivity or value-based-care incentive structure and want to gauge how likely it is you'll earn a top bonus (or none at all), you're likely better off asking the person who would be your supervisor or the administrator of the group.

In short: arriving at your interviews with thoughtful questions in mind, prepared to pose them to the right person at the right time, is both an indirect way of selling yourself and a crucial tool for deciding if a job is right for you. Don't skimp on this preparation.

Interviewing mistake #2: Not preparing for tough questions

Any job interview can be anxiety provoking. That goes double if you're worried about questions that could be uncomfortable.

Preparation can help tamp down those nerves—especially when your anticipation of a difficult question is what's revving them up.

For example, did you take a break during your training, leaving a gap in your CV—and are you wondering how that looks? Were you briefly employed as a physician, with nothing on your CV in the months since? Are you wondering how much you should disclose about a time when you had doubts about your commitment to becoming a physician, or a break you took for mental health reasons?

If you're worried that a gap in your CV might give a recruiter or hiring physician pause, and if it's not a sensitive personal issue, head off questions about it by addressing it in the cover letter or CV.

For example, if you took time off after a fellowship to travel or get married, or for some other non-private purpose unrelated to your career, there's no reason not to briefly mention that either on the CV or in your cover letter. Doing so won't just preclude the need to discuss it in your interview, it can prevent a busy recruiter or hiring physician from hastily putting your application aside because of the unexplained gap.

Similarly, if you're applying for positions that require board certification and you aren't yet certified but your exams are scheduled, say so.

If you're worried about more personal issues that could cause something in your CV to look "odd," prepare for how (and how much) you'll talk about it in an interview. This way, you won't be caught off guard or embarrassed in the conversation.

Remember, interviewers are unlikely to push for private details. Their concern will be whether the unusual pattern in your work history suggests that you might leave abruptly, be ineligible to practice, or have difficulty getting along with others. Unless the issues prevent your being licensed or insured or working successfully in the employer's environment, they're unlikely to be deal-breakers, and the employer probably won't push for details. A simple and clear explanation is usually all that's required.

And what if a conflict led you to leave your last job after a short tenure—or if you were asked to leave?

Again, preparing to discuss what happened helps head off stress. If you left because you were unhappy, frame the reasons as objectively and neutrally as you can. Avoid bad-mouthing your prior employer (and especially any former bosses or colleagues). The same applies if your exit wasn't your choice. Instead, focus on what you've learned from the experience, and how it's influencing your current search. Be honest, but don't elaborate where honesty doesn't require it.

Interviewing mistake #3: Misunderstanding recruiters' roles

Charlie Munger, the lesser-known investing partner of Warren Buffett (the very famous "Oracle of Omaha"), is often quoted as saying, "Show me the incentives. I'll show you the outcome." It's an idea I find useful in practically any business situation. Incentives can be complicated and multi-factorial, but they explain a lot of organizational behavior.

So, what does this have to do with physician recruiting?

While one recruiter's job title might sound the same as another, physician recruiter jobs actually fall into multiple categories. They're all paid by prospective employers[1], but the way they're paid influences how they do their jobs.

Take in-house recruiters, for example. The in-house recruiter is an employee of a hospital or health system. They're typically compensated (or at least mostly compensated) with a fixed salary. Though they're judged on how successfully they fill their open jobs, they're not paid per hire. How well new hires fit into the culture and their eventual longevity (or turnover) will be more important to them than to other types of recruiters, especially if their organization has been struggling with physician turnover.

Compared to external recruiters, in-house recruiters know a lot more about the jobs they're filling (after all, they're employees of the hiring organization). And they'll likely spend a lot more time getting to know you.

External, fee-based recruiters work for a recruitment company or agency (or sometimes as freelancers). Physician recruitment agencies break down to two common types: contingency and retainer-based. In both cases, the recruiter is likely working for more than one hiring organization at a time, and those organizations could be hundreds or thousands of miles apart. They could be very familiar with the employer, but it's also possible they won't know some (or even many) of the details about the hiring organization that you'll want to know.

A retained search recruiter is engaged exclusively to fill a job. They'll receive at least some payment up front (versus only getting paid when the job is filled). They typically have exclusive contracts, which means retained recruiters won't be competing with other recruiters to pass along candidates for interviews as fast as possible (a plus for candidates). Speed still will matter to both recruiter and employer, though. The recruiter still makes more money the more jobs they fill. And a retained recruiter feels pressure to prove they can fill a job better than a contingency recruiter, without sacrificing timeliness. They'll do a customized search, presumably learning more about the organization the longer they work together.

In many cases, if a retained recruiter does a good job for the employer, they'll have a long-term relationship and act almost as an extension of the employer's in-house team. A trusted recruiter may end up handling open physician positions for an employer for years.

By contrast, a contingency recruiter's pay depends entirely on filling jobs. The recruiter (or their firm) is typically compensated with a percentage of the new hire's annual compensation. Some or all of the recruiter's fee may not be payable at all until the new hire has completed a year or more in the job.

A contingency recruiter's incentives work against getting to know you well. They're always in a race to send as many candidates who meet the primary qualifications to employers as quickly as possible.

Consider that a single employer may work with more than one contingent recruiter, hoping to benefit from their competition with each other, knowing they'll only have to pay if one of the recruiters eventually delivers a new hire. Only some of a contingent recruiter's listings will eventually pay off, creating a "numbers game" that encourages the recruiter to work on as many jobs as they can, for as many employers as they can.

Recruiters also know that the same CVs sometimes end up in multiple contingency recruiters' hands, even though candidates are asked to sign exclusive agreements. So contingency recruiters assume that if they invest too much time in getting to know a candidate, another recruiter could put that same candidate's CV into an employer's hands first. Then if the employer ends up hiring that candidate, the recruiter who spent more time up front missed out on a hefty commission.

For you as a job seeker, the difference between these different recruiter types boils down to the quality of information they have about the job; their interest (or disinterest) in getting to know you; and their inclination and ability to negotiate on your behalf.

With in-house recruiters, you have the best shot at getting accurate and detailed information about the opportunity. Still, don't forget: they're recruiters, not physicians. If there seems to be a match, it's still up to you to pose all your detailed questions about office culture, the requirements of the job, day-to-day duties, compensation, and anything else you need to know to the right people in the organization. But an experienced in-house recruiter has spent a lot of time inside the organization, presumably working with lots of physicians and staff. They've undoubtedly picked up a lot of insight from that process. They're also likely to be most concerned with making a *strong* match. Beyond qualifications, they'll look for fit.

And what about discussing that offer letter? The in-house recruiter likely had a hand in preparing it, so if you have questions, they're a good person to start with. (If they don't understand the ins and outs of the compensation scheme, be sure you talk to someone who does.)

As far as negotiation goes, though, it's clear that the in-house recruiter is not on your side of the bargaining table. That means that as much as they'll want to hire you, they'll also be protecting the financial interests of their employer. Do your research about compensation in your specialty and get help from a professional that *you* pay in order to be sure you're getting as good a deal as possible.

With retained recruiters, there will be more variation, but if you're working with a recruiter who's enjoyed a long relationship with an organization and filled many of their physician jobs, their insights about what it's like to work in a particular hospital, group, or system will likely be similar to an in-house recruiter's. They may also have comparative information about other employers, though they're less likely to want to share that lest it turn your head elsewhere. Still, that comparative information could come in handy at negotiation time, when their insider knowledge could reassure you that an offer is market-priced, or prompt a nudge of the employer to increase one that's not. (This is not a substitute for doing your homework, creating your own negotiating strategy, and getting expert help if needed.)

With contingency recruiters, your expectations for details about the job or efforts they'll make to ensure you'll be a good fit should be low. If they happen to have information you need that could help you decide on whether the fit's right, that's a happy surprise.

On the plus side, a contingency recruiter has an incentive to get you a higher salary, since their commission is almost surely based on it. Remember that they also have a competing incentive to close the deal quickly, though, and the fact that they benefit from increasing your compensation doesn't guarantee that their knowledge of salaries in your market is current and accurate, since they could be recruiting all over the country simultaneously.

As you begin your job search and start responding to postings, it may not always be clear which type of recruiter you're dealing with. Of course, it's OK to ask. (Even when the recruiter explains a bit up front, it might not register at first. Ask if you're not sure!)

To be continued...

In the next chapter, three more categories—financial mistakes, negotiating and legal mistakes, and etiquette mistakes—round out the list.

CHAPTER 2: MORE MISTAKES JOB-HUNTING PHYSICIANS MAKE—AND HOW TO AVOID THEM

FINANCIAL, LEGAL AND NEGOTIATING, AND ETIQUETTE MISTAKES

Financial Mistakes

Financial mistake #1: Not comparing apples-to-apples

It's natural when looking for a job, especially your first post-training one, to focus on salary when comparing two opportunities. Anyone who's waited years to earn "real" money would have the same bias.

But when you're considering physician jobs, you'll typically be offered a complex mix of benefits that will also impact your financial position. Nailing down the value of all of them requires some persistence (and probably a spreadsheet), but it's indispensable if you're deciding between two otherwise similar offers and are using finances to break the tie. If you were to compare solely based on salary, it's easy to choose the less lucrative option accidentally.

For example, for each job you're considering, calculate how much you will have to pay (if anything) for licensing fees or malpractice insurance. Any portion of these expenses paid by your employer in effect increases your income. If your future employer offers disability insurance (almost always a must for physicians), will that offset some of what you'd have to spend?[1] Gym memberships and any other perks you could receive that you'd otherwise pay for should be included in your analysis.

Retirement benefits can also have a substantial impact on your finances. Plans vary widely, with the financial differences varying accordingly.

For example, if two jobs offer a 401(k) plan, but one offers a five-percent match (essentially, free money placed into your retirement account to match what you contribute) and the other doesn't, that's potentially a significant difference in compensation.

Health and life insurance also deserve scrutiny, especially if you have a spouse and/or children. Consider both how much you'll be charged for health insurance premiums and the cost sharing (deductible, co-insurance, copays, and maximum out-of-pocket). Will you have dental and vision coverage for the entire family? How much will this save (or cost)?

Life insurance is also important if anyone else is depending on your income. The amount of insurance provided in an employer's benefits package can vary significantly. Consider how much you'll have to pay out of pocket if an employer offers only modest coverage. (If the employer offers you the option to purchase additional coverage under the group plan, you may be able to do this through payroll deduction, pre-tax—another cost savings.)

You should also factor in whether any compensation or benefit dollars come with strings attached. For example, some retirement plans require vesting before the company match is earned. If that money won't actually be yours until you've been in your job for three years, consider how likely it is you will stay put for that long. Similarly, relocation packages and signing bonuses may have payback provisions if you leave your job before a milestone is met (commonly three years).

Financial mistake #2: Assuming the worst about productivity pay

Productivity compensation, with all its various models, terms, and permutations, can be complicated enough to deserve a whole book of its own.

But then again, the connection between productivity and your compensation is in many ways straightforward, and it doesn't deserve to create as much anxiety or confusion as it often does.

The connection between your productivity and your compensation may also be virtually unavoidable. Regardless of whether you have a productivity-based compensation plan or are on straight salary, your production will be important to your employer.

In most types of healthcare organizations, physician production pays most of the bills. That means your anticipated revenues will be part of how your pay is determined and part of an overall budget that keeps the organization in the black.

Even when your productivity is not explicitly used to calculate your earnings, it may be a factor in determining future salary increases or in calculating team bonus compensation. Productivity is also connected to an organization's ability to meet quality and social goals like providing as much community access to care as possible.

This may sound like common sense. But if we know that productivity will be assessed as part of every job (whether explicitly tied to pay or not), why does it sometimes cause anxiety?

Some job-seeking physicians have told me that they're used to understanding things backwards and forwards and then along comes productivity pay with a bunch of off-putting new terminology. This lack of familiarity may cause some of the productivity-related hesitation job-hunting physicians experience. Unfortunately, since the concept of productivity usually surfaces during the first-job search, when physicians are already super busy completing residencies and fellowships, it's also harder to find the time to bone up. Some doctors hope that a guaranteed salary will make it a non-issue.

Lack of familiarity may not be the only cause of hesitation around productivity pay, but it's a factor you can easily address. Business-side concepts may be new to you now, but none of it is as hard as you might fear (and maybe not even as boring). Besides, if there's anything every one of you reading this book excels at, it's learning things.

Chapter 12 is an easy place to start. It covers basic terminology and includes insights from colleagues who are further along in their physician careers. (There are entire books out there to read after that if you'd like to dig deeper.)

And what if the aversion to productivity pay is about something else? Other physicians have told me that the concept of tracked productivity conjures an image of a treadmill they can't get off. They wonder if it means the system is rigged, ensuring they'll earn less for the same work.

Unfortunately, I suspect this thinking leads to some physicians actually earning less because they are so biased toward guaranteed compensation and reluctant to have any pay tied to volume.

There is no doubt that the goals of some productivity plans are difficult, if not impossible, to achieve. I've encountered a few of those rigged situations in my consulting career. Though they are, I believe, relatively rare, it's absolutely essential that you do your own analysis of any productivity compensation you're thinking of signing on for.

On the plus side, it's much easier to understand (and compare) how physician pay works than in the past. The attitudes of many younger physicians (who aren't signing up for all-work-no-play—and good for them) and the ability to easily share data online have contributed to more transparency. This makes these impossible situations rarer simply because people can learn to avoid them. It's also just so hard to find good physicians that cheating them can't be very profitable over the long run.

Also on the plus side: Survey data shows that physicians generally make more when productivity is explicitly compensated[2] (whether as a bonus or 100% of pay). If you're rejecting productivity pay out of hand or hoping to minimize it, there's a good chance you're turning down additional pay before figuring out how hard it would actually be to earn it.

It's also worth noting that physician firings (or even discipline) for lack of productivity, at least in my experience, are pretty rare. In fact, I don't recall encountering a physician who was fired for productivity reasons in my (dozen plus) years of consulting work, even though physician productivity is usually something clients want me to analyze carefully.

When a physician's productivity is lower than expected, in my experience it's most often a scheduling, workflow, or marketing issue that's the reason. Addressing the drags on productivity usually makes it possible for the physician to see many more patients without adding stress. Or if the physician is new to full-time practice, they might need a bit more time, and perhaps some mentoring, to get up to speed.

So while I urge you not to reject compensation plans that include productivity outright, evaluating potential drags on productivity is essential. These are things beyond your control that could hinder your ability to reach productivity benchmarks.

Here are some examples of productivity-related questions to keep in mind as you're evaluating an offer/opportunity:

Is the productivity level I'm aiming for possible, given scheduling, workflow, and my job responsibilities?

- What will my schedule be—and will it maximize my clinic encounters or procedures? Will I even have enough OR time to achieve the volume needed? Is volume in my specialty predictable enough?
- Will I have enough staff support to keep patients moving through my day? For example, will I have a dedicated medical assistant (or more than one, if I can demonstrate that more support would make me more productive)?
- What is the EMR? What customizations are possible, and how much support is available? Are other supports such as virtual or live scribes an option? Are physicians currently completing their charts same day?
- If workflow problems surface (such as scheduling issues or clinic flow) that affect physician productivity, how are those addressed?
- Will my time be diverted to responsibilities that may cut into my productivity—for example, supervising non-physician providers? If so, will their production contribute to my goals?
- Do physicians typically make the productivity goals? If they don't, what are the reasons?

Are there (enough) patients waiting for me?

- Is this a new position or am I replacing a departing doctor?
- Is the exiting physician leaving a patient base large enough to meet productivity? If not, how many more patients will I need?

- If this is a new position to meet unmet demand, how was need determined? (How long are patients currently waiting for appointments?)
- If I'll be building a practice from scratch, how long before my pay depends on production?
- What kind of marketing support is provided to attract new patients? What type of marketing am I able (or expected) to do?
- How are new patients assigned?

How will I know if I'm on track to meet goals?

- Will I have access to current reports to track my billings and/or RVUs?
- If productivity pay will be based on net collections, what is the billing department's collections track record?
- How would I estimate my collections based on my charges?
- If I need assistance with or feedback on my coding, is help available to ensure my claims are paid?

These sample questions are, of course, a starting point! The idea is to identify factors that could help or hinder your ability to meet productivity goals, so you can assess how likely it is you'll meet or exceed them. Hopefully, this list brings other questions to mind, especially issues specific to your own specialty.

Another way you might think about productivity pay: as a trade-off of risk and reward.

For both you and your employer, the decision is really about trading off certainty and financial risk. If you're able to take on more risk yourself—bet on your own productivity—you may be able to make more money.

Consider the employer's point of view. They know that the market for your skills is highly competitive. Employers know they have to pay enough to attract you—and, hopefully, to keep you happy. Once they've attracted you, retaining you is their next objective, and that's going to be much harder to do if you feel underpaid.

But budget concerns are very real, too. If your employer guarantees more compensation than your revenue supports, it could invite serious financial trouble (especially if it does this over and over again with all physicians in the organization).

That's why some employers will offer you significantly more potential compensation if you choose more productivity pay. By tying all or part of physician compensation to revenues they generate directly, employers shield themselves from financial risk. If they know they're putting less money at guaranteed risk (by waiting to be sure you generate it), they're willing to pay you more of what you produce. This is because they know that doing so won't push them into the red[3].

Your situation is the mirror image of the employer's.

If you're very risk averse (say, because of a student-loan burden), you may have a strong preference for predictability (ideally 100% guaranteed salary). You may feel prepared to forgo some potential upside in return for that predictability.

This is a perfectly rational way of looking at your compensation. It may be precisely right for you and your situation. The critical thing is to assess the financial trade-off as objectively and accurately as you can.

Whether you're giving up any upside (and how much) will depend on the details of the productivity plan. That's why it's so important to look closely at the math when evaluating a productivity plan. Calculate the RVUs or charges that would put your compensation on the same track as the guaranteed pay option. It's possible, even likely, that the risk is lower than you're assuming. (It may be that you hit the same pay at a pace you're already comfortable with.)

You should also calculate how much more you'd earn by working slightly (or not so slightly) harder. Would it be enough to justify the additional risk? The answer will vary based on your situation and personality.

Of course, it bears repeating that for most people, money isn't the only important decision factor. Consider all the intangibles when evaluating a productivity plan that might give you only a small compensation edge.

One final thought on productivity: if you're loath to dig into productivity calculations because you find the whole subject too tedious or feel you just don't have time to learn what you need to know, there are compensation experts who can help. Money invested in these services can repay itself many times over.

Legal and Negotiating Mistakes

Legal mistake #1: Not getting the right help

The most harmful legal mistake I've known physicians to make is simply not having legal help (or the right legal help).

The documents a prospective employer presents to you will have been written by an attorney with the employer's interests in mind. You should level the playing field by having an experienced health-care attorney in your corner. The costs of this are probably less than you expect, and, in any case, are likely small compared to the possible costs of signing an unfavorable contract.

The second, avoidable legal mistake is waiting too long to find your attorney. Line up an attorney who suits you before you start receiving contracts (or even letters of intent), so that you'll have the help available to quickly analyze any offers you're considering. This way, you won't have to plead with prospective employers for more time to decide while you scramble to find an attorney (or worse still, attempt to do without one). You won't be rushed in your work with your attorney, either.

The attorney you hire should be experienced in physician employment contracts, preferably in the location where you are planning to work. Local knowledge is valuable partly because the attorney may be familiar with how physician contracts have evolved in recent years in the market, so they may be able to comment on whether your deal is structured comparably or suggest whether and what you should try to negotiate. Your contract may also include some terms that are valid in some states but not others—another way local legal expertise is invaluable.

Non-compete agreements, for example, are increasingly scrutinized in many states, and even outlawed in some[4]. Where contractual requirements like non-competes, no-poach, and other restrictions are allowed, their potential effects on you as an employee will depend on numerous factors that the attorney can help you weigh.

An attorney experienced in physician contracts can also help you avoid the common mistake of signing a document you don't fully understand by ferreting out and correcting ambiguous, confusing, or one-sided language.

For example, if you ask the employer about a section full of fuzzy legalese, you may hear the phrase "it's just boilerplate," meaning that some of the language of a contract is standard and typical of physician contracts. This may or may not be true, but you still shouldn't sign it without knowing what that "boilerplate" language means. An attorney will help you do so and push back on terms that are too broad or inequitable.

Your attorney can also help you confirm that key sections of the agreement, such as how compensation is calculated, reflect what you understood from conversations with the employer. (If you've hired a compensation consultant, as mentioned in the previous section, their advice about the clarity and competitiveness of the compensation structure will also be invaluable.) Your attorney will also notice if needed terms like dates, termination rules, dispute resolution, and malpractice coverage are included and appropriate.

If you inquired about a special consideration during your interviews and the prospective employer agreed, but then you find it's missing from the contract, your attorney can help you draft an amendment to suggest to the employer.

It's not unusual for special conditions to be mistakenly forgotten and omitted from contracts. The reasons can be benign. During the process of preparing offers for multiple candidates, customizations can be overlooked, and the person writing the contracts may not even have been party to your interviews. Just be sure you remember to take notes during your interviews and/or save copies of important emails and texts between you and the people you meet with. Your notes will help you remember the verbal agreement and help your attorney draft an addition to the contract to propose to the employer.

Legal mistake #2: Hoping for the best (without planning for the worst)

As a consultant who typically works with physicians who are years into their careers, I've seen the impact of this mistake too often.

Though you may get the impression that contract terms are squishy, or that in the future you'll be able to renegotiate restrictions that don't matter to you now, it's critical to assume that any contract you sign will be enforced.

Some of my clients have found deeply disappointing surprises buried in contracts they signed years ago. It can happen when you try to switch jobs locally or, especially, start a practice of your own.

When contracts signed a decade or more ago interfere with your current career and business plans, the pain can be anything from inconvenient to costly to downright heartbreaking.

Some of my clients had hoped the excellent relationship they built with an employer over many loyal years would allow them to negotiate some of the pain away today. Unfortunately, I've never seen this happen. If the contract terms you want to change are favorable to your employer, your employer will almost certainly enforce them.

This is why—though admittedly it's difficult—you should try to project into the future when evaluating employment contracts. At the very least, don't ignore the future effects of restrictions in the contract simply because you don't need more flexibility now. (This is yet another way an attorney experienced in physician contracts can help you.)

The importance of restrictions is more easily spotted in some cases than in others.

You may already be on the lookout for non-compete provisions, for instance, as they've gotten a lot of media and legislative attention in recent years.

There are other terms, though, that even if confirmed or revised in ways helpful to you, may be less likely to catch your eye. Or perhaps you're unsure about whether it's worth trying to negotiate —a question I advise you to think through as carefully as you can.

For example, employers often seek to prevent exiting physicians from recruiting colleagues or even staff to a competing employer (or a competing practice those physicians might want to start). Broadly written clauses about the ownership of patient records and your rights to communicate with patients after you leave may not seem important now but could be extremely important down the road.

Even if you're not contemplating starting a practice now, is it out of the question in the future? Negotiating away as many of these restrictions as you can before signing—with the advice of your attorney—can keep your options more open in the future. (The fewer restrictions on your ability to inform patients about your change of practice, the better your next employer will like it, too.)

Termination terms are another restriction that can pinch in the future. How much notice will you have to provide if you decide to leave? How much notice will you get if your employer decides you should?

The bottom line is, if you find yourself dismissing certain language in the contract because you can't see it applying to you (at least in the near term), wait a beat. Make sure your attorney has helped you understand anything that isn't perfectly clear. And spend some time thinking through restrictions that aren't relevant today but could impede your future plans.

Related advice: DO NOT[5] lose track of your contract documents.

When you make plans for a career change or a new business in the future, you will need to know what you signed. You won't want to be reliant on the other side—possibly now an adversary—to provide you with the document. Consider, for example, a situation in which your employer is letting you go. Do you want to rely on them to produce a copy of the executed contract so that you can confirm they're living up to the provisions intended to protect you?

Another reason to make sure you can always easily access your contract is that laws change. Some important restrictions (like non-competes) may be less enforceable or even illegal in the future. When considering a change in your work life, legal review of what you signed by a trusted attorney can help ensure that your understanding of your rights and obligations is up to date.

Negotiating mistake #1: Narrow thinking

You probably already know that it's a mistake not to negotiate for things that are important to you. It's expected in a job-offer situation. But negotiating isn't only about your wish list. Considering only what you want and not the other side's perspective is a common mistake.

Knowing what the other side values is one of the best ways to strengthen your own position. Keeping your requests reasonable and bringing data to support them is always a better idea than just "shooting for the moon" with no logic behind it. And combining your request with something the other side values will greatly increase your chances of success.

For example, a straightforward request for a salary increase might prompt a quick "no" from the employer. But if you're prepared to offer something in exchange, such as adding some unpopular hours to your schedule or providing more vacation coverage, that might justify the additional pay you're after. (Similarly, if you really want something that an employer might find difficult to accommodate, such as a specific schedule or less call time, your chances could improve if you accepted a lower salary or other concessions.)

It's also important to recognize that sometimes "no" is the only possible answer and not indicative of disrespect or a failed negotiation. For example, large employers often have compensation structures that are specifically designed to ensure fairness and market competitiveness. Even if the hiring manager wanted to honor your request for more money, that simply might not be feasible.

But even when it seems the employer can't be flexible, consider whether you can. A bit of creativity and some pre-planning might keep the negotiating door ajar. For example, when a salary increase isn't possible, more money for relocation costs or a higher signing bonus might be.

It's also a common mistake to think of negotiation as mainly about compensation, but this type of tunnel vision can be costly. Successfully amending other terms of the contract, with the help of a lawyer, could be more valuable to you in the long run.

Negotiating mistake #2: Failing to prioritize

Even in the most flexible and ideal situations, you're unlikely to get everything you ask for. Be sure you know what's most valuable to you.

Your fit with the culture, for example, or a location where your family is looking forward to setting down roots could be worth much more than a minor difference in salary. Don't let small disappointments in negotiating terms cloud the bigger picture.

Being prepared, prioritizing your goals, having some win-win options in mind, and being professional and gracious are invaluable ingredients in an employment negotiation. Keep in mind that if it's a job you want, the people you're negotiating with will become your coworkers.

Etiquette Mistakes

Etiquette mistake #1: Undervaluing etiquette

"Etiquette" sounds like it deals with niceties—feel-good actions that are relatively inconsequential. But when it comes to job hunting, the reasons to care about etiquette are very practical. Even when you're in very high demand, people notice the considerate choices you make (or don't make). People care, and they remember.

Some etiquette choices matter more than others. If your CV is on a job-search database and a recruiter from an organization you're not interested in contacts you, you're unlikely to suffer consequences if you ignore the message.

But if you send a quick message stating that you're not interested because you're aiming for a different type of practice, that can only help your image. The recruiter now knows they've reached you and won't need to keep trying. You've saved them time by being considerate, which they'll appreciate. And who knows? That may smooth the way for you to contact that recruiter in the future (if, for example, you decide you'd like to work in their type of organization after all).

Another way to show consideration (and interest) is to research the people you'll be meeting with. You'll ask better questions, your prospective colleagues or bosses may be flattered or impressed, and your interest will be clearer. Perhaps it's not a deal-breaker if you don't do it for each person you'll meet, especially if your specialty is in high demand. But the interview will be better for both sides each time you do.

Once you've had on-site meetings, the etiquette stakes get a little higher. Take the decision whether to send a thank-you email. It's a good idea to do it, and not just to be polite. Thank-you notes reinforce your interest. If you don't send them, the recruiter or hiring manager may wonder how interested you are. That's an inconvenience to them, especially at the later stages of interviewing, that's easily avoided with a quick email. (Templates are available online to speed things up.)

Generally speaking, the further you get in the process, the more impact consideration (or lack of consideration) has. Once you reach the offer stage, a breach of etiquette can lead, at least indirectly, to suboptimal employer decisions that even affect other people.

Imagine a situation in which you're offered jobs by more than one hospital. It's easy to happily share your "yes" with the one you like best, but less fun to tell the others you're turning them down. You hesitate... and before long, you've procrastinated into the common-but-avoidable gaffe of never officially declining the other jobs.

Once you've ignored a couple of emails from the recruiter "just checking in," maybe you start to convince yourself that the recruiter surely must have figured out that you're not joining. Don't listen to that little voice. Ghosting in this situation is not just rude, it may create bigger problems for the organization.

Consider the possibility that you were their first choice. That would almost surely mean they've held off offering the job to other candidates while waiting to hear from you. But if they delay offering the job to other qualified physicians, those other candidates could also accept jobs elsewhere. The hospital could miss their chance to hire anyone this season and wind up short-handed.

This potential for serious inconvenience is one reason why people remember when candidates do this.

And here's the thing: if you're going to be working in the same town, you'll likely be connecting with the people you met during your interviews again. Sometime in the future you might even decide you'd like to work at that organization after all. When you decide you want to build out your network or look for a new position, it will be a lot easier if nobody remembers you as that person who left everyone hanging after being offered a job.

You may be thinking that job-offer situations won't always be as easy to manage well as the one I described—if so, you're absolutely right. It's unlikely you'll receive offers from all the organizations you're interested in at exactly the same time. When you've received or are waiting on offers (plus engaging in negotiations), timing differences can make the etiquette of communicating with prospective employers tricky.

For example, what do you do if you're offered a job but were hoping to hear from another employer before deciding?

The good news is that prospective employers assume you're talking to multiple organizations, and they know you're in demand. It's OK (and polite) to let the employer who offers first know you'll need more time.

If you can avoid it, though, it's best not to reveal a rank-order preference. If the employer realizes they're not your top choice, that could make them less excited about your candidacy. They might wonder whether, if you were to eventually accept, it would mean that you were settling, or that you'd be more likely to leave in a year or two.

Explaining that you are "hoping to hear back from a couple more possibilities before deciding" is information enough to be truthful without inadvertently hinting that you prefer another option. Expressing that you're just doing your due diligence shouldn't ruffle any feathers, especially if combined with a sincere reiteration of your interest in their job.

Of course, employers are usually eager to receive your decision as soon as possible, so being prepared to complete any legal or compensation review promptly so that negotiations conclude quickly will be appreciated. As already mentioned, if you've planned ahead and lined up your attorney and other advisers in advance, you'll need less time to deliver feedback about the offers you receive.

One more tricky bit of etiquette: dealing with reference requests. Once you get to this stage, you'll need to be considerate of the people who've agreed to speak for you. Give your references notice of who will contact them, and spread the burden out so that no one gets too many calls.

Having reference letters available may make some conversations superfluous (or more productive). Most important: don't list references on or with your CV. Instead, hold them until an offer is imminent and you feel positive about the prospect of accepting one.

CHAPTER 3: MISTAKES RECRUITERS AND EMPLOYERS MAKE—AND WHAT YOU CAN DO ABOUT THEM

Does the title of this section seem a little odd? Should you care about mistakes that are completely out of your control?

Mistakes made by people you meet during the recruiting process won't always be things you can (or should) do anything about. But when others' errors could lead you to a bad decision, put you in an awkward situation, or set you up for a bad start in your new job, it's worth trying to recognize what's happening and respond in your own best interest.

Unrepresentative gaffes

A few years ago, I was assisting a client with recruiting for a partner-track allergist position in a desirable part of the country. The practice owner had received the CV of a promising candidate. He asked me to interview her, tell her about the practice (I knew it well, having worked with them for several years), and set her up for a visit. He wanted her visit to include not just interviews, but also a chance for her to observe the workflow and experience what a "typical day in the office" was like.

This was music to my consultant ears. The job would have a heavy productivity compensation component, so I thought it would be very helpful to this physician to see the practice's efficient and well-staffed workflow in action.

When I explained the process to the candidate, though, I inadvertently used a word that was loaded for her: "shadow."

I can't recall what else I said. I only remember that the candidate became quite offended. To her ears, my suggestion that she'd be "shadowing" implied that I didn't respect her many years of successful practice.

The worst part (aside from realizing that something intended to benefit the candidate had come across as an insult) was that no amount of explaining or apologizing on my part seemed to repair the damage. The incident evidently left a terrible taste in the candidate's mouth. To her, my silly error apparently reflected a disrespectful attitude on the part of the employer.

The frustrating outcome of my mistake was a loss for everyone. The practice missed out on the chance to hire a needed physician. And by overestimating the meaning of my error, the physician missed out on a great chance to one day own a highly profitable practice.

I'm sure it's obvious that I learned not to use that word again in an interview! But I think there's something job-seeking physicians can take away from my experience, too.

Recruiters and others involved in hiring physicians, especially at the early stages of the process, are not likely to be physicians themselves. It's easy for them to bungle in ways that would probably never happen in physician-to-physician communication.

Maybe you're thinking you'd never react similarly in that particular situation (as some physicians have told me). But there are all kinds of ways in which a non-physician could goof up and say something that reveals they don't understand your experiences at all.

So: my advice is not to infer too much from the goofs of laypeople —or anyone, really. If you find yourself believing you've just picked up a clue to a troubling hidden issue in an otherwise appealing opportunity, check the validity of your reaction by talking with others and asking questions. And be sure you're asking the right people—i.e., the ones you'll work with every day, not the recruiters or HR people.

Recruiter overselling or misinformation

When you're in the opposite interview situation to the tense one I just described, and you're enjoying a breezy conversation with a recruiter who answers all your questions with just what you want to hear, you should be just as analytical. Because while it's delightful to hear that the culture in the pulmonology group is "fabulous" and "fair," if the recruiter can't reference any particular aspects of, say, how call is assigned or regularly reviewed for equity, odds are good he or she's blowing sunshine up your skirt.

Recruiters are highly motivated to fill jobs. Depending on the type of recruiter, sometimes they literally have no other goal beyond putting a breathing M.D. or D.O. into an open position. If the recruiter is not rewarded for ensuring you're a fit for the culture or the location, they're less likely to admit that they don't really know how "great" the job is on the particular dimension you're asking about. (Maybe they don't even know what they don't know.)

A recruiter motivated to "just fill that job" with any qualified physician is behaving rationally, given the incentives of their job. But those incentives could lead the recruiter to make mistakes that affect both the employer and you. When physicians are hired into jobs that aren't a good long-term fit, both the employer and the physician lose.

Even in-house recruiters who are prioritizing long-term fit may find that their incentives subtly change as your candidacy progresses. If you've impressed everyone and the hiring physician has decided they really want you, that in-house recruiter could feel more pressure to make it happen—and be more likely to lean toward blandly reassuring answers to your questions about your prospective daily work life.

Your solution to their mistakes? Don't rely on recruiters for answers that you should be seeking from prospective colleagues, your future boss, the practice administrator, or others more qualified to provide the information.

Leaving key questions unasked

One of my consulting clients, a mid-sized practice owner, called me recently to start a search for a new physician. He explained that a series of mistakes had led to an expensive exit for his newest M.D. hire.

This M.D. had started with my client's practice as a locum tenens. The practice CEO suggested to the owner that they make a permanent offer to the temporary physician. While they'd have to guarantee several months' pay to the locums agency, this would likely be a lot less expensive and labor-intensive than starting a fresh search. It seemed like a perfect solution for everybody.

But once the physician started full-time, minor problems surfaced. He had moved from another part of the country and a different type of practice, and his style was out of step with the culture his new employer had established and with the community vibe.

The practice owner now had to decide whether to let the physician go (absorbing the cost owed to the agency as a consequence) or try to mentor the physician and help him adapt to the practice culture and local expectations.

But while in the process of deciding, the practice owner discovered something a lot more problematic: the physician wasn't board-certified. Somehow, no one had checked to see if he possessed this important credential.

As you're likely aware, board certification isn't always necessary, but my client's malpractice policy requires it. Therefore this physician simply shouldn't have been hired in the first place.

Now the practice owner had no option but to let the physician go immediately. And he was still stuck paying that huge agency fee, even though the physician couldn't work for him to help earn that money.

Of course, the situation was just as bad for the physician, who now faced the frustration, pain, and financial cost of being fired. In all likelihood, he'd also have to move again, quite possibly at his own expense, or return to itinerant work providing temporary coverage.

It's probably clear that both the recruiter and (especially) the practice CEO screwed up. The CEO assumed that the locum tenens recruiter had checked for board certification. He had another opportunity to confirm that with her before making the full-time offer, but he didn't do so.

For her part, the recruiter could have predicted that board certification might be important, since it often is. Perhaps she avoided the issue for fear of scuttling a lucrative placement. Given that the practice paid her employer a huge cancellation fee, it's safe to assume she got some kind of commission, despite not doing her best by the physician or her practice client.

And what about the physician himself? That's more to the point of this book, after all. Could he—should he—have done something to prevent this costly snafu?

Misunderstandings about credentials are, unfortunately, not uncommon. The further along in the hiring process, the more costly they are for all involved. So I say yes—you should be proactive about avoiding this kind of situation, even if it really shouldn't be your responsibility.

Consider that as a candidate, you're investing your own precious time (and perhaps your limited paid time off) whenever you interview for a job. If you spend any time at all interviewing when your credentials don't match up with, say, strict employer requirements for malpractice coverage, insurance credentialing, or privileges at a hospital or surgery center, you've wasted something scarce and valuable to you.

When in doubt, it's always better to bring up what credentials you currently have and what you expect to have (by what date) if the recruiter doesn't think to ask you about them.

Recruiter omissions that affect you can happen with details unrelated to your clinical skills, too.

For example, some recruiters may not think to ask if there's anyone else who will be a part of your decision to relocate or who should attend on-site interviews with you (such as a spouse or partner). Maybe they'll assume you'll speak up if you want to bring your partner along, or maybe they're leery of asking too personal a question. Then if you also find it uncomfortable to ask, a crucial issue goes unaddressed.

If something you think is important (whether to your decision or the employer's) hasn't come up in your conversation, raise it yourself.

It's unlikely that simply asking for, say, the option to bring your spouse to a site visit; the chance to speak to a physician who's currently in a similar role; or the option to talk to an administrator or staff about clinic flow will cause offense, even if the employer ultimately has reason to say no. This will be true for most honest, well-intentioned questions. (And if the employer were to be turned off or alarmed by such a question, that's probably something you're better off discovering before you consider joining them.)

Overtaxing your references or inadvertently sharing identity data

In other places in this book, I've advised that you handle your references with extreme care. Providing references is time-consuming. You don't want the time of the people who've kindly volunteered to vouch for you to be wasted or abused.

Maintaining strict control over your reference list is also the best way to minimize the risk of a recruiter or hiring physician mishandling your references.

Don't add reference names to your cover letter or on your CV or even as an attached list, even though it seems more efficient. There's too much risk an overzealous recruiter (or a physician who recognizes someone on your list) will contact them prematurely. The last thing you want is for a recruiter from an employer you're not seriously considering to squander a reference's time and goodwill!

Instead, maintain a complete list of references for your own use, but don't distribute the whole thing to anyone. (If you provide all of them, the recruiter will likely contact all of them, not just the ones you'd like them to.)

At the appropriate time, provide the prospective employer a customized subset of contacts. Check in with those people, too, to be sure it's still OK to name them as references—and let them know who will be contacting them. This should be when you're near the offer stage (at that point, most employers will need to check them) and only if you're seriously considering joining the organization.

Until then, if you're asked about references, employers won't usually expect contact information, though they will want to confirm you have references ready. (A simple "I'll be able to provide several" should suffice.)

If you're already employed, there's another reference-related recruitment error to be aware of.

Sometimes, a person you meet with may realize they know your current boss or other person you work with and spontaneously contact them for a chat about you. This mistake could be very awkward for you if your boss is unaware you're looking for a new job!

To prevent this, make sure people know that your job search is confidential. (Using a personal email for job hunting will reinforce this point and will keep anyone who has access to your work email from noticing job-search activity.)

Besides omitting references, you should also keep financial identi-fication information like your age, maiden name, or Social Secu-rity number off your CV and cover letter. Remember that a recruiter is unlikely to check for a potential breach of financial data before freely sharing your documents. Yes, this personal data will likely be needed for a background check, but you can share it at the offer stage, and usually you'll be given a secure way to do so.

Unshared assumptions

In my work with consulting clients, one of the most troublesome hiring mistakes I've witnessed is when newly hired physicians and the people who hired them discover too late that they have completely different ideas about building a new practice.

Trouble can bubble up if the hiring physician assumes that the job applicant has a similar set of assumptions about how to build up a practice. Often, though, the hiring physician has been in practice for multiple decades and hasn't had to do any personal marketing for a long while.

One case I remember involved a rheumatology practice owner who was looking for a new grad to join him as an employee, help build and expand the practice, and then take over when the owner retired (expected in about five to ten years). Rheumatologists were in short supply in the very desirable location of the practice. The set-up was a fantastic opportunity for a new hire with an interest in practice ownership.

After a national search, the practice owner found a physician to join him who seemed absolutely perfect. She was completing a prestigious fellowship and very much looking forward to joining the practice, helping to grow it, and eventually buying it from the owner. Everything appeared to have worked out ideally.

When the younger physician started, though, the practice owner quickly became disgruntled with her marketing methods. All he could see was that she didn't spend any time at the hospital glad-handing other specialists or doing lunch-and-learns—the bread-and-butter marketing methods that he'd always relied on.

The new hire *was* marketing herself, though. Instead of focusing on the hospital, she was quietly building her own local network, doing small-group presentations at local offices, and developing her online presence.

The new hire's steps were excellent, modern ways to gain referrals —in fact, in the current market, her ways were more productive than the practice owner's hospital-focused approach. The practice owner didn't appreciate how much referral channels had shifted since he had begun building his business (more than thirty years before).

To make matters worse, the owner's taciturn personality meant that he never discussed his concerns with the new doctor, nor had he ever discussed with her his assumptions before she was hired. (Later, he would admit that he simply thought they were every-one's assumptions!)

Instead, the owner grew quietly frustrated and resentful. To him, if his new doctor wasn't spending time at the hospital schmoozing, she wasn't putting energy into marketing—and that meant she wasn't committed to the practice.

Unfortunately for the practice owner, he wasn't able to get past his resentment. He and the new hire parted ways within a year or two of her start date. (Though the experience was a painful one, things worked out fine for her eventually. She decided to strike out on her own. Solo practices can be tough to pull off, but it helps when you're in a specialty with long patient wait times and have already made progress in building your referral network.)

There are loads of ways this problem of differing assumptions can affect your understanding of your new job. For example, if you ask during interviews "Is call shared fairly?" you might get the (honest) answer "Oh yes, of course." But does "fair" mean the same thing to you and the person you asked?

I've worked with clients who were mystified by the poor morale of their youngest colleagues, who were expected to handle all of the most difficult work and the worst schedules. The younger doctors' reactions were amplified because they had been told things would be "fair" — but it never occurred to them to ask for a precise definition of the word. To the hiring physicians, shifting the night work onto newbies was perfectly fair since that's how it had always been done.

Maybe it shouldn't be up to you to sniff out these unstated assumptions, but if you are to avoid these types of problems, you must. Remember, too, that once the specifics are revealed, you may have an opportunity to negotiate—yet another reason for specific questions and clarity.

The key is to make sure everyone is truly on the same page. Once you've already signed a contract, it's likely too late (or at least it will certainly be much harder to successfully renegotiate).

Another area where hiring physicians and organizations sometimes unintentionally err: on-boarding.

Generational differences in assumptions can cause a lot of trouble here, too. Back in the day, it may have been perfectly reasonable to throw a new physician into the deep end of the pool without a lot of direction (or "hand-holding").

But back in the day you also might not have had such steep productivity goals to meet. On-boarding—the process of acclimating you to everything about the job—should be the process that helps ensure you can meet those goals.

So ask about on-boarding—about who will help you learn the lay of the land, get up to speed on productivity and technology, and master other critical things you'll need to know.

Be sure you get specific details. I once met a candidate who savvily asked about on-boarding when considering joining a relatively new private group. The candidate worried, correctly, that the group had no coherent on-boarding plan. But when the candidate asked his intelligent questions, the owners immediately realized that they'd failed to adequately plan for an introduction that would set their new hire up for success. That candidate helped ensure not just that he got off to a good start, but that every other physician the group hired in the next few years did, too.

PART TWO: PLANNING AND PREPARING

CHAPTER 4: WHEN (AND HOW) TO START YOUR PHYSICIAN JOB SEARCH

It's Almost Never Too Early to Plan

If you're a current resident or fellow, you may have heard from colleagues that you should start applying for jobs in your final year of training, since that's when job postings proliferate and organizations get serious about hiring decisions. Yet if you ask a physician who's recently completed a job search, or a mid-career physician, or a program director who works with graduating physicians, you might be surprised to hear them recommend starting your job-hunt planning much earlier.

"I remember being told 'six to twelve months' [ahead of graduation] was the time to explore what's out there," says Alexandra Ristow, M.D., a primary-care physician in Tampa, Florida. "But given the constraints of residency, earlier is better."

Vivian Hernandez-Trujillo, M.D., FAAAAI, FACAAI, FAAAP, fellowship training program director of allergy and immunology at Nicklaus Children's Hospital in Miami, Florida, says that she's noticed a need to plan earlier that began with the pandemic. "Normally, I'd say six to nine months would be OK, but now I say at least nine to twelve months out. Everything is just very fluid."

Today's job-seeking physician is well advised to start at least a year out, ideally even sooner—both to avoid being unduly stressed by combining a busy residency with job hunting, and to better navigate the shifting sands of the physician employment market. Starting earlier can help ensure that you make the best, most informed decision you can make.

If you've been thinking about the job search as a process of applying for postings and completing interviews, this advice may seem confusing. Why start job hunting before you can actually be hired? But the extra planning time experts recommend is not primarily for responding to ads or submitting applications—it's for research and preparation that will arm you to search more effectively and choose your first job more wisely.

Pre-search planning and preparation (timing: from medical school on)

Thinking about your first job when it's years away might seem wasteful, especially considering that med school and residency are so demanding. But there are things you can do when you first start training that will help smooth and support the more active part of job searching that comes at the end of your training. Accomplishing certain tasks earlier will make the more intensive, interview-focused portion of your search easier. What's more, starting early is an opportunity to build assets and skills that will help you throughout your physician career.

One thing to consider early on is where you'll want to live when you launch your career. Many physicians find it comes naturally to locate in the same metropolitan area where they do their residencies. "There's good and bad about [this tendency]," says Gus Geraci, M.D., FAAFP, FAIHQ, a family practice physician and healthcare consultant, referring to the mix of factors that leads physicians to favor staying put where they did their residencies. "The good news is that you'll know the area, and you'll know many physicians." But the bad news, he says, is that depending on your specialty, there might not be many opportunities to change employers later. This can be frustrating if you discover your first job is not a good fit, or if you don't like the area of the country well enough to stay for the long term.

If you can land a residency in your preferred location, that's ideal, but this is often not possible. "It's the match system. You open the envelope and that's where you're going," says Ristow, acknowledging that residents often must compromise on location to pursue a particular training program. Still, even if you can't be sure you'll secure a residency in the market you hope to set down roots in, thinking about your geographic preferences before or early in your residency is invaluable. If you know for sure that you'd prefer a different location post-training, you can build connections during residency that can help when you're actively job seeking down the road.

These early contact-building efforts don't have to provoke anxiety. In fact, they can be much more natural than what "networking" normally implies. Getting started can be as simple as using social media sites like LinkedIn and Facebook to stay in touch not just with colleagues in medicine, but friends from college and even earlier in your life. This way, if you find you prefer a different location after your training, you'll know who among your connections has already landed there.

Expanding your network is a daunting aspect of job hunting for many professionals, not just physicians—and it can take a lot of time. Developing this skill early can make it easier. Building connections through social and learning opportunities helps you meet like-minded people and can be more comfortable than trying to find appropriate contacts and ask them for help when you've already started applying and interviewing.

One way to start early is to get involved with causes and organizations you care about. "I used to do a lot of interfaith work and held a lot of leadership positions in college," says Atena Asiaii, M.D., MPH, an OB/GYN with El Camino Medical Associates in Mountain View, California, noting that exploring personal interests can help physicians focus "on the diseases and patients you feel the most passionate about treating."

Specialty societies offer many opportunities for med students and resident physicians to make connections in a way that feels frictionless. Often there are free conference tracks for med students and residents, as well as job fairs—great opportunities to network and learn about practice options. You may also find opportunities to take on a leadership role in the society—perhaps representing students in the specialty or doing a presentation at a conference.

"With the help of the AMSA [American Medical Student Association], I did my first poster as a med student," says Hernandez-Trujillo. "It's never too early to start giving back," she adds, noting that sharing and helping others is one of the most powerful ways of networking, especially for physicians who may be uncomfortable asking for help or putting their career goals first.

Hernandez-Trujillo also points out that physicians who go on to specialty training may have the option to join multiple societies—in her case, she is a fellow of the AAP [American Academy of Pediatrics] as well as the AAAAI [American Academy of Allergy, Asthma & Immunology] and the ACAAI [American College of Allergy, Asthma, & Immunology]. All offer her the opportunity to stay in touch with colleagues and make new connections.

Another job-search task you can start very early on—during medical school or when starting residency—is drafting your initial curriculum vitae (CV). Draft the basic document and it's a simpler matter to update it with new credentials and publications as your training progresses—eliminating the need to put valuable job-hunting hours into creating a CV when you are ready to apply for a position. (If you don't have a template, Hernandez-Trujillo says, check in with your program director, who probably has one that's a good fit for your specialty.)

Explore practice settings and learn practice management basics (starting with residency)

The CV is one documentation task that can be a hassle if you wait until it's needed for potential employers. Another is tracking the procedures you'll be accumulating in your post-med-school training. Future employers will need documentation that you've completed the requirements for hospital privileges, and it's much easier to track that as you go than to tally years' worth on the fly.

Your specialty society may have an app you can use to track your procedures, says Poonam Velagapudi, M.D., M.S., FACC, an interventional cardiologist and associate program director of cardiology fellowship at University of Nebraska Medical Center. "But you can do it in a Google Doc if necessary."

Tracking your work accomplishments and productivity has another advantage. It can help you build an understanding of the economics of medicine. If billing and coding training is offered during residency, pursue it early on. Adding learning about the economics of medicine to the demands of a busy residency may seem excessive, but trying to do it while juggling interviews and evaluating offers will be even harder. Starting earlier makes learning at a more manageable pace possible.

Besides the essentials of billing and coding, learning how benchmarks and productivity work can help a physician compare compensation plans more accurately when the time comes to evaluate offers, Asiaii says. She did multiple job searches in the few years after her training—and learned from each search and each position. Among many observations, Asiaii learned to ask about productivity expectations, because a job that appears to pay more may actually pay less on an hourly basis.

Geraci points out that there are books you can turn to to learn the basics of physician compensation. And organizations like the Medical Group Management Association (MGMA), plus the practice management wings of specialty societies and medical associations, offer surveys, webinars, and other tools.

Learning about the business side of medicine can also help you evaluate practice settings—another key decision you'll have to make. For example, Ristow says she began learning about alternatives to fee-for-service medical practice from a senior resident who told her about value-based care practice groups he'd learned about. Without base knowledge of billing and productivity terminology, it's harder to compare alternative models and determine what setting is ideal for you. Starting this research earlier in your residency will enable you to learn about more options and narrow them at a manageable pace.

Your fellow residents, especially those ahead of you, and your program director can be invaluable in helping you explore your practice priorities and options. There's no downside to building these relationships with trusted colleagues and potential mentors as early as possible.

"I met some of my mentors through ACAAI and AAAAI," says Hernandez-Trujillo. "They were able to help me to progress not just into my first career positions, but also into leadership roles." Most important, she says, is that your mentors know you personally. "They can say, 'I can see you fitting in here.' Or, 'I have a friend who's hiring and I want to recommend you.'" Building trusted relationships like this takes time.

Velagapudi adds that residents and fellows who need a visa to work in the U.S. should research what practice settings will be open to them, based on the type of visa they hold. "Reach out to someone ahead of you. A senior fellow or colleague who has dealt with that can help." Lead times for visa paperwork can be long, too —another reason to learn what's required before the customary "nine months to one year" job-search timing you might assume.

Go time! (one year out)

With one year until the end of training, it's time to get into the thick of the job search. A key place to start is creating online profiles and signing up for alerts, not just with independent recruitment sites, but also from the job boards offered by specialty societies and journals.

It may feel a bit early, but you're likely to see at least some postings for your specialty, as Hernandez-Trujillo points out, because some organizations will want to make hiring decisions that far in advance. And you will have the chance to put some of what you've learned through your research and mentor relationships to use, refining your preferences and priorities.

Doing your best in your interviews also means preparing. That can take the form of role-playing with fellow students or more experienced colleagues. But you want to be sure to prepare not just for the interviewers' questions—you want to prepare to ask your own.

"My biggest takeaway from the job-hunting experience, both right out of residency and again a few years later, is that you need to approach it with the mindset of creating a partnership," Ristow says. "You won't get an offer from every single job. It's most important to get the job that fits you."

Ristow believes that medical training, with its emphasis on competing at every stage, can condition physicians to want to please everyone. "But if you go into an interview and come out saying 'I nailed it, they loved me,' but don't have the info you need to decide whether the job is right for you, you've failed."

She adds that while physicians might hesitate to ask about organizational culture and clinical philosophy, these questions are usually regarded as a sign of engagement and preparation. More important: If you don't ask these questions, and you wind up in a position that doesn't fit your practice goals, that's a lose-lose for both you and the employer. Adds Asiaii, "If they're going to reject you for your curiosity about the job, it's probably not the right one for you."

At the same time, understand that the process is akin to a courtship. "You don't want to lead off with questions about compensation," says Velagapudi. It's best to start off with more general issues and work toward the specific when (and if) it becomes clearer to both sides that you might be a good fit.

If you're searching in a smaller subspecialty or region and are seeing few posted jobs, you also may find you're not getting as many interviews as your peers. It's not cause for alarm or discouragement: You just may need to do more legwork.

"Call the local medical society in the area you're targeting and tell them you're looking for a job in their area. You'll either get 'no' or you'll get 'you should talk to so-and-so, they're looking,'" says Geraci. He points out that not all jobs are advertised—especially opportunities with smaller practices. If you're hoping to work in that type of practice, don't be surprised or discouraged when there are fewer such jobs posted. There may be opportunities you can dig up through your own networking efforts.

Hernandez-Trujillo echoes this advice about reaching out, adding that "even if someone's not hiring now, they might be a few months later."

When you reach out to a local organization or a prospective employer and find there's no opening on their radar at the moment, they may also refer you to someone else who could be hiring. Being polite and thanking everyone you meet with or who helps you can ensure that you're remembered positively if an opening arises in the future.

If you find that your efforts to drum up interest aren't yielding many (or any) interviews, you may have to consider whether your target is too narrow. "Make a list of your priorities," says Velagapudi. "There may be one or two that are really important for you. They are your soul. The others, you should be willing to compromise on."

Before you get too far into the interview process, you should also be sure you've lined up the reference letters you'll need. "You don't want to have to give people a one-week deadline," Velagapudi adds.

As the process unfolds, you'll also need to prepare to negotiate. At the early stage of applying and interviewing, you still have time to read up on the language of negotiating and seek advice from mentors and colleagues.

Homing in on a choice (six months or less until decision time)

As you get closer to follow-up interviews and offers, it's time to be sure all of your questions have been answered, and that you're armed to negotiate and evaluate offers.

It's a good idea at this stage to line up professionals who can help you review any contracts you're considering. Says Geraci, "Have your contract reviewed by a health-care attorney experienced with physician contracts—not a general business attorney." Some organizations may ask physician candidates to sign a preliminary document, such as a letter of intent, before moving ahead with a contract—and your health-care attorney should review that, too.

Connections you've made with residents who've gone on to employment ahead of you may help with finding the right attorney. And rest assured, Geraci says, that you can probably work remotely with the lawyer, so you should be able to find qualified advice even if you're searching in a remote area.

Spade work done earlier in your residency to learn about physician compensation structures and productivity metrics will serve you well now. But if you haven't yet got a handle on these things, it's time to dive in—or look for help from a consultant who specializes in evaluating physician contracts.

Your questions of would-be employers should get more granular now, too. If you'll be compensated all or in part based on your productivity, ask about factors that help or hinder it, like the support staff you'll work with, the marketing investment to support building your practice, whether productivity is based on RVUs or net collections, and whether there is an existing backlog of patients.

Asiaii recalls that one of her early jobs paid very well, but with that higher compensation came productivity expectations that were difficult to meet. When she was searching for her current job, she applied what she learned, asking questions that made the employer's expectations much clearer.

"I didn't know what questions to ask at first. This time around, I wasn't shy about it," she says, "I asked specific questions, like 'What if I can't get my OR time?', 'How many patients will I be expected to see in a day?', and 'What happens if I don't meet my benchmarks?'"

Besides compensation questions, job seekers should explore the culture of any group or institution they're considering joining. Asiaii says that, as an OB/GYN, she needed to ask if any procedures are off limits. All physicians will want to understand the schedule in detail, and those who will be on call will want to make sure they're clear on how those responsibilities are scheduled.

Getting a clear picture of the practice culture also means talking to people working there—and not just the ones tasked with hiring.

Brooke Grant Jeffy, M.D., FAAD, a dermatologist in the Phoenix area, recalls that during the interview process for one of her first career positions, "they flew me out to visit, but I was very sheltered from other physicians." She now considers this a red flag and encourages younger physicians to be sure they can speak to doctors who would be their colleagues before deciding to accept an offer.

Adds Velagapudi, "Ideally you'll be able to visit in person to talk with many people—not just physicians." She points out that staff members have a valuable perspective and can help you get a feel for the work environment.

Your second job search—and beyond

Even if you do all your homework and ask all the right questions, it's possible, perhaps even likely, that you'll be ready to look for a new position a few years after you start your first one.

"Most of the people I trained with stayed in their initial practice about two years. You're just lacking in preparation for how to look for a long-term position," says Jeffy, who adds that physicians looking for their second position are much better equipped to know what they will like or dislike about a job.

All of the advice about thinking through your preferences and being unafraid to ask specific questions still applies—and the good news is you'll be much more knowledgeable about what type of practice setting will be your best fit. And if you've been maintaining and expanding your network, it will be a more valuable asset to your search.

Businesspeople whom you will meet through your work—for example, drug and device reps—also may have the inside scoop on practices that are hiring and what the atmosphere is like there, adds Velagapudi.

Social media also has a useful role for physician job seekers. "There are all these Facebook groups for physicians only now," Jeffy says. "I moved across the country and looked for another job without any contacts [with the help of people in these groups]. In smaller specialties, everyone kind of knows everyone." She also says that the ability to communicate through private Facebook messages is invaluable, because you can ask colleagues pointed questions without posting them publicly. Jeffy adds that, if possible, it's helpful to track down physicians who've left the practice, to talk with them about their experience. This can be harder to do, but Facebook and, especially LinkedIn, can help.

Geraci reminds young physicians hunting for their first job that keeping options open for their second is one reason why having an expert legal review of your contract is so important. Some contracts will include covenants that aim to prevent you from competing with your employer if you decide to leave, Geraci points out. These can restrict your ability to switch jobs in the same community, or even start up a practice of your own. But with your attorney's help, you might be able to amend these terms to make them less restrictive, or even negotiate them out of your contract altogether.

A shorter version of this chapter appeared as a feature in PracticeLink magazine's Spring 2021 issue, along with the timeline that follows.

CHAPTER 5: JOB-SEARCH TIMELINE

A Rough Timeline of a First-Job Search

Early in residency, or even in medical school

- Consider the area(s) where you'd like to live and practice
- Establish and update your web of connections—personal and professional—on social media
- Get involved with your specialty society(s), AMSA, or other professional groups
- Start learning about practice options

During residency

- Draft a CV you can update as you go (track procedures, too, if needed for your specialty)
- Get to know your program director
- Make connections with senior residents and prospective mentors

- Learn more about your preferences and goals
- Gain basic knowledge of medical economics (RVUs and productivity, coding, payment models)
- Stay active with your specialty society (for example, by attending job fairs)

About a year from graduation

- Sign up for job boards and alerts
- Gain more information about practice settings you're drawn to
- Plan and practice for successful interviews
- Solidify your priorities, deal-breakers, and nice-to-haves
- Study up on negotiation techniques (or take a course or get a coach)
- Reach out to local medical associations and societies for connections and possibly unadvertised openings
- Make sure your ducks are in a row with respect to administrative tasks like visa paperwork (if applicable), reference letters, and procedure documentation

Six months or less from graduation (decision time)

- Ask to visit any organization you're seriously considering, if you haven't yet
- Meet your prospective colleagues and staff
- Line up legal and business help for reviewing contracts
- Get answers to your detailed questions about compensation, work life, and culture

CHAPTER 6: WRITING YOUR CV: WHAT TO SAY AND HOW TO SAY IT

At its core, a medical CV (curriculum vitae) is simple in concept: it's a factual, chronological inventory of a physician's credentials and experience. Yet when the time comes to prepare and submit your CV to potential employers, even this straightforward definition may leave you with questions—and it should, because even though a CV is uncomplicated in concept, how you prepare yours can make a big difference to your job search results. A well-done CV can help open doors to the places you want to go; a CV with avoidable mistakes may keep them closed.

Refining your CV—settling on a format and carefully determining what to include and omit—is an important early step in your career search. It can be time-consuming, perhaps even a bit tedious, especially when compared to accumulating more medical knowledge as you approach the end of your residency or fellowship. But the extra time it takes to perfect it is worth it.

"The CV's the one thing that the practice you're interested in is likely to see about you [to help them decide whether to meet you]. Think about how much effort you've already put into premed, medical school, your boards—you've put in all of this work toward your medical career, over many years. And now, whether or not you land that crucial interview all rides on your CV," says Ben Kornitzer, M.D., chief medical and quality officer of agilon health in Boston. "It's what will help you get that dream job you've worked so hard for. Putting in the extra effort to get it right really matters."

CV versus Resume: Tomato, Tomahto?

If you've previously prepared a resume (for, say, a summer job or a previous business career), you may think you're halfway to your CV. But while these documents serve similar purposes, there are important differences between them.

With a resume, there's more stylistic flexibility. Candidates just starting out might even opt for a "functional" or "skills" resume that broadly describes traits, interests, and accomplishments instead of a chronological work history. This deliberate downplaying of the minimal work experience of candidates just starting out is acceptable in many business situations. Business candidates are also expected to "sell themselves" by burnishing their brands in their resumes. But in medicine, objectivity and clarity about credentials and experience are paramount—and even a whiff of "embellishment" could backfire.

"[Business resumes] use catch phrases and imply skills and motivation to entice the prospective employer. It can become nebulous," says Robert Marinaro, M.D., FAAD, a dermatologist with US Dermatology Partners in Sherman, Texas, and Richardson, Texas. "But a physician CV should be really cut and dried."

Whether the goal is to practice as a clinician or use medical training in a business setting, Marinaro adds, the "creative language" that's customary on business resumes would be far too unclear for a physician candidate's CV. "Even if you're applying for a pharma job, you want to know that the person reading it can cut through the fog [and understand your credentials]."

Where a CV is much more flexible than a resume is its length. It's unusual for a resume to exceed two or three pages, even for long-tenured business professionals. An overly long resume may even hurt a business candidate's chances. But CVs expand as needed to include all the publications, credentials, and awards a physician has accumulated over the course of their career—which can yield very lengthy CVs, especially in academic medicine.

John Madden, M.D., Wilmington, Delaware-based associate dean of students, director of the office of career guidance and student development at St. George's University in Grenada, West Indies, says, "When I advise students to work on their [first] CVs, they sometimes tell me, 'I've already got a resume.' I say, 'You need to create a *curriculum vitae*. Your resume is one page. I've seen CVs of departmental chairs that are 100 pages, because of all the publications.'"

Generally speaking, and especially if you're focusing on an academic career, a long and complete list of your publications, awards, credentials, and experiences will help make your CV more impressive. Still, outside of academic and hospital medicine, hiring physicians and recruiters say that length for length's sake is not an asset —and that aiming for a more compact, targeted document may be a good idea.

"You have to understand your audience," Kornitzer says. "If you're talking to a private practice, you may want to give them a very succinct, two- or three-page resume. But if you're going for a hospital or academic setting, you absolutely should keep the longer form [of a CV]. For most people going into non-academic medicine, though, the CV will be relatively short."

Gary Pinta, M.D., CEO of Pioneer Physicians Network in Akron, Ohio, adds that if you're hoping to land a job in a private medical group, a long bibliography might even send an unintended message.

"Long lists of publications are nice for academic settings, but if you've got twenty or more papers listed, I don't know if that makes a difference to us [as a private group]," Pinta says. "It actually might imply you're not interested in seeing patients all the time, or that you might intend to leave to teach at a medical school."

Culling work experiences outside of medicine also helps make evaluating your CV easier for the reader, who might be a professional recruiter and not a physician.

"[Even] for someone coming right out of training, I'm not looking at prior work history unrelated to the medical field. You can omit your service industry positions," says Marissa Phillips, physician recruiter for US Dermatology Partners in Dallas.

Madden agrees. "A CV shouldn't include experiences further back than college, unless those experiences are truly exceptional [and relevant]," he says. "If you were a landscaper in college, you don't need to list that. But if you did medical records or were a scribe, that's worth including," especially for the first CV you create for residency applications.

Resumes also customarily include a personal statement or objective at the top. This isn't customary in a CV, and some experts think it's unnecessary. Madden, for example, says, "That's a business thing. In medicine, I think everybody's goal will be to find a great job working with great people, providing excellent patient care." He also asserts that you don't need to state an objective because you're expressing your interest clearly by applying for a particular job.

But others argue it's a resume custom worth borrowing, because it can be an efficient way to communicate the type of situation you're looking for—a helpful signal to hiring physicians and recruiters.

"A brief headline of who you are can be really powerful. Practices want to find someone who's a good fit and will stay for the long run," Kornitzer says, noting that employers are concerned about the high cost and disruption of physician turnover.

For example, Kornitzer adds, since his organization is building a total-care model of primary care for seniors, "If someone put 'fellowship trained geriatric physician who is passionate about value-based care, quality, and outcomes' at the top of their CV, that would be exciting for us."

Pinta echoes this thinking. Entrepreneurship, a desire to lead, and interest in practice ownership are key things he's looking for when hiring physicians. Pinta says that a personal statement (or objective) on the CV emphasizing these things can indicate a higher likelihood of a match.

"If candidates say that they want what we have, then I know they understand what the job is. If you're looking at jobs and like a certain type of job, go ahead and say that it's your objective or vision. Then [the hiring physician will] know that you know what you're looking for."

Your CV Tells a Story

Adding an objective or personal statement is one way to shape the impression your CV creates. Another is through the details you include beyond the essentials. Optional elements help flesh out the story your CV tells: not just your credentials, experience, and accomplishments, but your path as a physician, how you've focused your energy, and intangibles you want potential employers to know about you.

For example, if you did volunteer work or research while you were still exploring the possibilities of medicine and discovering your interests, it may make sense to omit these experiences if they don't support your current interests and plans. On the flip side, if you had an entry-level job or a volunteer stint in an organization that's directly related to your current goals, it could be worth including, even if it happened before or during medical school.

Similarly, if you're applying for a position that would require a relocation, including a home address in the city you're targeting will make clear you have local ties, even if it's been a long time since you've lived there.

A thoughtful trim of your publications can also help keep the focus on the ones that tie most clearly to the work you're hoping to do.

Vanessa Hettinger, a remote recruiter out of Boise, Idaho, with Wilderness Medical Staffing of Spokane, Washington, points out that it's simply not feasible for a busy recruiter to review every publication in an extensive bibliography. Editing down to just the ones that best show off your expertise ensures they won't be missed, she says.

Kornitzer likens the idea of curating the optional information in a CV to how people tend to their social media: It's about what you choose both to include and leave out. "Your CV absolutely must be accurate and truthful, but at the same time, it should highlight those aspects of your background you want other people to focus on—just like with Facebook and Instagram, where you post when you are dressed your best or your kids are being really cute. You only have a page or two to convey what you want people to know."

Format and Content: The Essentials

Of course, while your CV tells a story, it shouldn't *literally* be a story. While it's natural to want to stand out by deviating from the norm, anyone requesting your CV will expect certain formatting standards. A little flair is good—but if your approach is too unexpected, your strengths could get lost. And if it's too off-the-wall, your CV could even attract the wrong kind of attention.

"I have received CVs that were formatted as an autobiography," says Phillips. "While this is a unique structure for a CV, I've found it hard to follow and not a good tactic."

And when it comes to fonts and other stylistic decisions, she adds, "Despite what you may see online, you don't need to have the prettiest CV, with graphics and different colors, to be noticed. Keep your CV simple and easy to follow, ensuring that you highlight your accomplishments."

Classic fonts like Times New Roman and Georgia that are known for readability are always a safe bet; using 12-point, if possible, helps ensure the text is easy on even the most tired eyes.

Instead of a narrative format, a CV should follow a relatively simple, outline-like structure that includes:

- Name and medical credentials (e.g., John Smith, M.D., or Jane Jones, D.O., FACOG)
- Contact information (address, phone, email, plus links to a personal web page or LinkedIn profile if you have one). If you are not a U.S. citizen, you may wish to add information about your work authorization status.
- Professional statement or objective (if you choose to include one)
- Academic rank and position (if applicable, including dates)
- Military service (if applicable, including dates)
- Schools and degrees (listing all institutions and start and end dates)
- Internships, residency, fellowship (including all institutions and start and end dates)

- Certifications and licensures (including dates and states where applicable)
- Work history (including start and end dates, and brief descriptions of your duties)
- Awards, honors, grants, and memberships
- Publications, presentations, research, and related activities
- Personal activities and interests

It's likely your CV will initially be scanned by a recruiter who is not a physician—and this person may be reviewing dozens of CVs every day. That's why it's so important to put your credentials, and especially your contact information, front and center. Training and experience typically appear next.

Actual dates for your education, work history, certifications, and licenses are essential. And while there's no hard-and-fast rule about where to place them, "dates lined up on the left side make it easier to scan," says Madden.

It's also best to use *reverse* chronological order for dates.

"Physicians will often list work experience beginning with their first job and ending with their most recent. [But to enable] us to make a quick assessment of whether a physician is qualified for a particular position, they should list their most recent job first, then work backward in time for every subsequent position," says Hettinger.

When describing job duties or other academic/career highlights, use short sentences or fragments, and maintain a consistent "parallel structure" – i.e., use the same type of grammatical construction throughout the document. And be sure to be specific, especially if you're targeting your first job after residency or fellowship.

"[New graduates, residents, and fellows] often omit specifications regarding what their job duties were. We need to know what they did on a day-to-day basis, what procedures they can perform, and what type of scenario it was performed in... so we know what they're capable of," Hettinger says. "It's helpful if physicians list their credentials and certifications in their CV. For example, if they have completed an ATLS course, that should be included, as well as the expiration date. Additional qualifications [like these] can make a candidate stand out."

If you're still working on a particular certification or credential, it's also a good idea to mention that, along with the anticipated date of completion.

Usually, not all the sections included in a template or CV guide will apply to every physician (including the list above). So, of course, omit those that don't—and feel free to present your publications, honors, memberships, and personal information and activities in the order that best suits your purposes. For example, if you have personal interests or traits that you know are important to a prospective employer, such as technology skills or bilingualism, there's no need to relegate that information to the bottom of your CV.

If you've been in practice for many years post-residency or post-fellowship, you may also prefer to list your education after your credentials, training, and work experience, since these will likely be of greater importance to a potential employer.

Simple Ways to Help Recruiters Help You

Your CV will likely travel from an email inbox to a recruiter's desktop and then be circulated among physicians and perhaps others in the practice. You can make it easier for everyone in the chain to use your document by setting up your file thoughtfully.

"Always save your CV as a PDF to ensure all parties are able to open the attachment," says Phillips.

To help the recipient easily save your CV and find it again on their computer, avoid using a filename that's meaningful only to you (like "my CV 2021"). Instead, include your full name and credential, and a date if helpful for your own version control (e.g., "John James MD CV December 2021").

Take care, also, to include full names of terms alongside acronyms or abbreviations that might not be familiar to a recruiter. And remember that the first reviewer of your CV might not even be a human being.

Hettinger says that "CVs are often run through software" that helps recruiters spot qualified candidates—one more reason physicians should include details of their job duties for each position on their CV. "If physicians don't list relevant keywords that could match them to available positions, our software might not signal that they are qualified for the position."

Remember that your CV will probably be printed at some point, too. "Put page numbers and your name at the top of each page of your CV, in case they get separated," Madden says. He adds that you should also print copies of your own—on high-quality paper —before attending a residency fair, career fair, or other event where you'll meet recruiters.

For CVs you'll hand out in person, Madden adds, it's useful to include a photo, since it will help recruiters remember you when they scan through the stack of CVs they'll receive at an event.

"In business, many people advise against including a picture, because you could potentially be discriminated against. But medicine is different," he says. "Besides, if someone would discriminate based on a picture, would you really want to work for them?"

Marinaro notes that if you decide to include a photo, be careful about the choice of which photo to include. The wrong kind of photo—too casual, too intimate, or too outdated—can send the wrong message.

"A picture may be helpful if you're flying in from out of state, so they know who they're looking at, or if they're picking you up from the airport," Marinaro says. "But it should be a professional picture with standard expected attire—your white lab coat with your name on it."

Easily Avoidable Mistakes that Grate

If there's one thing everyone agrees will needlessly hurt your chances, it's typos in your CV. Yet they still happen far too often, recruiters and hiring physicians say.

"I have received many CVs that had simple misspellings that I will correct before distributing the CV to our team," says Phillips. But it's a gamble to count on a kind-hearted recruiter to help you fix these errors, so be sure to run spellcheck at a minimum.

Ideally, though, you'll also do a review beyond spellcheck to root out problems it can't catch, like missing words, misused homophones, and inconsistent structure.

"Medical training frequently doesn't emphasize writing skills as much as other graduate disciplines. With physician notes, no one cares if there's a run-on sentence or typos, but in a CV, it looks really sloppy," adds Kornitzer. "Get another set of eyes—or a few sets of eyes—on your CV before you send it out. You want it as buttoned up and professional as possible."

Enlisting the help of friends with good grammar and proofreading skills can help. And before you send it to them, and especially before you send the final version to recruiters, another good trick for catching slippery errors is to read the CV aloud. You can also use the read-aloud feature of Word to read the document to you.

Another common mistake: using "Dr." before your name, instead of your name followed by M.D. or D.O. This could make it harder for the institution to verify your credential.

"I think podiatrists and veterinarians do this because people don't know what a D.P.M. or D.V.M. is," Madden says, adding that this wouldn't be an issue when applying for a physician job. Worse still: using both Dr. and M.D. or D.O. in your name, creating a redundancy that will irritate readers who know the difference.

Personal Details Can Help—But Tread Carefully with Some

"I like when people include personal interests," says Pinta. "Then when I meet them, it gives us something to talk about."

Hiring physicians mostly agree that including personal interests like hobbies, fitness activities, or travel adventures can foster rapport in the interview process. But another thing most agree on is that certain personal details may be too delicate, controversial, or otherwise problematic to add to your CV.

For example, while religious affiliations may constrain your availability to work certain schedules or your ability to perform certain procedures, it's likely best to save these concerns for the interview. If the position you're applying for has inflexible requirements, the employer should mention these in the job posting. And if there is flexibility, you will be in a better position to ask for it when it's clearer that you're a potential match.

Similarly, you may be tempted to add salary expectations to your CV. But at the application stage, you are unlikely to have any details about the compensation structure, which will provide context for the pay offered. And if you're considering multiple geographies, your salary expectations may need to vary based on location. Bottom line: waiting until it's clear that there's mutual interest will put you in a better negotiating position.

Some experts advise including a list of references on your CV, but this could cause problems if some references are contacted too frequently. And if you're currently employed, says Marinaro, a premature reference check by an overeager recruiter could lead to your "confidential" meeting getting back to your employer, putting you in an awkward spot at work.

"Have a half dozen professional references available to vouch for you, but don't include those in the CV," Marinaro says. Instead, wait until you're asked for references, ideally at the last stages of the interview process, when you're sure you want an offer. Then choose the two or three from your list who best match the prospective employer's likely questions—and alert them they'll be contacted. This provides the employer the background they need while ensuring that your references' willingness to help you isn't abused.

Mind the Gaps

Including accurate dates for all educational, credential, and certification attainment, as well as work history, is non-negotiable. Unfortunately, this also means that if there are unusual gaps in any of these, recruiters and hiring physicians will notice them and have questions.

Phillips advises candidates to explain any gaps in education or employment history in their CVs.

Kornitzer agrees that you should be prepared to explain any gaps but suggests that not all timing anomalies should be explained in the CV itself.

Some reasons for time off—such as maternity leave, medical leave, or a research opportunity—will be perceived as benign or positive.

These are easy to concisely explain in a CV. But what if you took time off because you had doubts about your specialty, or even your decision to pursue medicine? Kornitzer says that complex, personal issues like these are better explained in a cover letter—or perhaps better still, during your interview.

Start Early—Update Continually

You likely prepared a CV as part of your residency application process, but that document shouldn't gather dust until you're ready to search for a job.

"We reach out early if we see potential. We recruit starting year one of residency, so I think residents should have a CV in year one and build on it as they go," says Pinta. "We have recruiting dinners a couple of times a year, and sometimes include PGY1s."

Pinta adds that if they invite a resident to a recruiting event and they're already prepared with their CV, it sends a message that they'll also be prepared in their job.

Keeping your CV up to date is much easier than waiting until you need it, Kornitzer adds. "You should be updating it constantly. Otherwise, you'll find it hard to remember, 'What talk did I give last year? Was I on a committee? Did I sit in on a podcast?'"

Updating regularly also allows you to tweak the content so that your CV remains targeted to your current job goals. And that can start with formatting—since the style you used in med school may not be quite right for the jobs you're now applying for.

Developing the habit of regularly updating your CV won't just make your first job search easier, Marinaro adds. You'll want to keep it up to date even after your career begins, so that you can respond promptly to opportunities that come your way.

"You'll always need to have your CV ready. There's always going to be a situation where someone will say, 'I want you to be on a speaker bureau,' or 'I'd like to add you to our medical advisory panel, can you give me a copy of your CV?'" Marinaro adds that you'll also need a current CV for administrative purposes, such as applying for a medical license in a different state.

A shorter version of this chapter appeared as a feature in PracticeLink magazine's Spring 2022 issue.

CHAPTER 7: SIMPLE STEPS TO A SUCCESSFUL COVER LETTER

Too many physicians assume—perhaps encouraged by job boards that make it simple to shoot your CV to a recruiter—that writing a personalized cover letter is unnecessary, even a waste of time. But would it surprise you to know that I've personally worked with practices that won't consider candidates who don't take the time to write an introductory letter?

I'm not just talking about small private practices, either. I've talked to senior hospital executives, hiring physicians, and long-tenured health system recruiters, and almost to a person they've told me how important those introductory letters are.

If you have any doubt about whether it's worth the time to write them… *it is!* Especially since it needn't take very long once you get the hang of it.

Why cover letters matter

It's no secret that physicians are sought after and in short supply. It might seem odd, then, that organizations desperately needing physicians would reject candidates for such a seemingly trivial reason. But recruiters, hiring physicians, and practice owners look to those letters for important clues about you.

Cover letters reveal hints about whether you've done your homework about the organization and the local market. Done well, they convey your genuine, informed interest to an employer.

Knowing that your interest is sincere and well-founded is almost as important to an employer as knowing your qualifications. That's because practices, hospitals, and health systems aren't just looking to fill a job with any qualified physician. They want candidates who will be happy and who'll stick around for a while.

After all, physician turnover is one of the reasons the market is so competitive. Plus, as a new physician, you'll need time to build your practice. Unless you stay at least a couple of years, it's unlikely the organization will recoup their investment in hiring you. Even experienced physicians will need time for their practices to become profitable in a market that's new to them.

How well you'll fit in an organization largely determines how likely you are to stay. Fit involves a number of factors, like how well-suited the organizational culture is to your personality and ideals and whether the type of career paths the organization provides match your goals.

For example, if the practice has spent years building a team-based culture that doesn't use individual bonuses to reward personal productivity, they'll want to know not just that you're comfortable with this model, but, ideally, that you're looking to practice in this type of culture. A teaching hospital might want to know you're excited by its longstanding reputation and the culture of innovation and learning it fosters (especially since its salaries might be lower than the salaries of non-teaching competitors). And a Catholic hospital that operates under the church's Ethical and Religious Directives will prefer to interview candidates who are already aware of these rules and prepared to practice under them.

In addition to work-related factors, wise recruiters know that in order for you to be a good match for the job in the long run, your significant other and family need to thrive in the community, too.

One of my clients here in the San Francisco Bay Area looks specifically for evidence of a past connection to Silicon Valley or the Greater Bay Area in a cover letter.

While everyone knows that Northern California offers incredible natural beauty and lifestyle amenities, my client's worried that candidates and their families will recoil from sticker shock at the prices of houses (and pretty much everything else) in this expensive part of the country. He's learned his lesson from losing several employed physicians after just a year or two for this very reason. Now when he needs to hire, he prefers to leave the job open rather than bring aboard a physician who can't prove they already know what it's like to live here. (You could imagine recruiters and hiring physicians having similar concerns about candidates who'd be relocating to locales with extreme weather or rural hospitals in quieter parts of the world.)

Which brings us back to those cover letter clues. In just a few sentences, you can convey that you've learned something about the employer that prompted you to write. You can make clear that you're familiar with the area and excited about the prospect of living there. By doing so, you immediately increase your appeal to the employer.

Cover letter basics

Your cover letter doesn't need to be complicated or thousands of words long. In fact, it should be no more than about a page (two to three hundred words). And you can almost follow a template to make it simpler to customize them for each employer.

Keep in mind that your cover letter will accompany a copy of your CV, so there's usually no need to repeat details that are laid out in that document (unless you're explaining or amplifying or connecting a detail to your interest in the employer).

Instead, you want to focus on your specific reasons for applying for the job (or to the organization, if you're inquiring about a possible position that you haven't seen advertised).

Your letter should address up front any concerns you expect the employer might have when considering any candidate (such as the location or type of practice). And you want to share some of your personality, any personal connections you have to the practice, and why you'll be a great fit.

For example, did you learn about the employer (and the aspect of the practice or job that attracts you) from a physician who works there or an adviser in your fellowship program? That's worth mentioning right up front.

Just as with your CV, save your letter as a PDF to ensure it's always readable (you can paste it into your email and attach the PDF). And you'll want to make sure your contact information is easy to spot on your cover letter. (Right under your closing is convenient.) This helps in the event that your letter and CV are printed and inadvertently separated as they're shared among people involved in hiring. (Remember to include multiple ways to reach you—email, phone, text—since the person you're writing to will have their own preference.)

To aid the reader, if you're applying for a job you saw posted, reference the exact title, location, and job number (if provided) from the ad. Be sure to address your letter to the right contact's name.

If the name is not provided in the posting, you'll probably be able to track down the name of the practice administrator, managing partner, or owner (for an independent practice) or the medical director, department chief, or recruiter (for a hospital or integrated system) with a quick Google search or scan of the organization's website. (Sometimes, if the information's not readily available online, a quick phone call will do the trick.)

Sample structure[1]

Salutation:

[recruiter][Dear Ms. Evans,]

[practice owner][Dear Dr. Collins,]

[practice administrator][Dear Ms. Jones,]

Introduction:

[I'm writing about your open oncologist position (physician job #12345), which I saw on the doc-needed.com website... I had been hoping to speak to someone at YourCancerCenter about possible openings, so I was delighted to see your posting....]

[I'm completing my rheumatology fellowship at Chicory Medical Center in New Orleans soon, and Dr. Shine, our department chair and my mentor, suggested I get in touch with you about possibly joining your practice....]

[I'm writing about your posting of an allergist position on the AAAAI website... I'm a board-eligible pediatric allergist completing training this year (including taking my boards in September). I'm specifically searching for employment as an allergy and asthma specialist in YourTown....]

A few specifics:

[Naturally, I'm drawn to YourCancerCenter's unsurpassed global reputation, but I'm also interested in the position for personal reasons. Through my fellowship (and my prior experience as Chief

Resident), I've come to realize I have a strong preference for academic medicine. YourCancerCenter's affiliation with University of MyState, would allow me to pursue my passion for cancer care in a teaching environment close to my home....]

[Dr. Shine mentioned that you're looking for a rheumatologist who is interested in building up a new practice and helping you and your partners expand. She added that YourCity is experiencing a severe shortage of rheumatology care (like so many places), and that you are considering hiring non-physician providers as well, to extend the reach of your practice. I'm excited by the opportunity to help you efficiently serve more patients and am very committed to building a busy practice in YourCity....]

[I'm very impressed with your use of technology, including telemedicine, to extend access to allergy and asthma care to more rural areas outside of Sacramento. (I learned about your innovations through June Caswell, executive director of your local medical society.) I'm passionate about finding new ways to bring asthma care to more children, especially in underserved communities....]

Closing:

[I've attached my CV and a copy of this letter. I'd welcome the opportunity to speak with you by phone or in a virtual interview. My contact information appears below....]

[I've attached my CV and a copy of this letter. I'd welcome the opportunity to speak with you by phone or have a virtual interview (with you or with your designee). My contact information appears below....]

[I've attached my CV and a copy of this letter. I'd welcome the opportunity to speak with you by phone or in a virtual interview. Or if preferable, I will be visiting the Sacramento area from

XX/XX through XX/XX, as my fiance is interviewing for jobs there as well. My contact information appears below....]

Signature:

Include your contact info, for example:

Melinda Jones, M.D.

Title/specialty

PGY [name of program]

Name of department

Email address:

Cell:

Final thoughts

Once you've gone to the trouble to prepare your custom cover letter, do your best to keep typos and clunky grammar from tarnishing your first impression.

 Ask your spouse or a friend in your residency program to read your letter for you (perhaps you can trade off that chore). There are also excellent electronic tools to help, such as ProWritingAid or Grammarly's free version. Text-to-speech, another reliable (free!) way to catch pesky errors like missing words, is available in Word and Google Docs.

PART THREE: FINDING YOUR FIT

CHAPTER 8: EMPLOYMENT VERSUS PRIVATE PRACTICE: HOW MIGHT YOUR CHOICE AFFECT YOUR QUALITY OF LIFE?

Once upon a time, most physicians came out of medical school with plans to own practices.

"That's how it was when I was growing up," says Leland Rosenblum, M.D., ophthalmologist and owner of Monterey Bay Eye Center in Monterey, California, and co-owner of Monterey County Eye Associates in Salinas, California. As a child, he had a private-practice role model in the family: his grandfather, a family physician who owned a practice in New York City. Rosenblum recalls that owning a practice was the norm, and employment less common, until "around the mid-90s, when I came out [of training]. At that point, physicians started to look at employment differently."

Fast-forward to today and young physicians aren't just open to employment, they undeniably tend to favor it—especially when starting out. In fact, in a 2019 survey by Merritt Hawkins, 91 percent of residents said they'd rather be employed than in independent practice. The same survey found that 43 percent of respondents preferred salaried hospital employment—the single most popular option. And only 7 percent and 2 percent, respectively, said they preferred a partnership with another physician or setting up a solo practice.

Whether because of a desire for financial stability, increasing consolidation of practices in health care, or the option to bypass the details of business management, more residents today are leaning toward salaried positions. But if this tendency to prefer employment at the beginning of a career leads to ruling out practice ownership altogether, will physicians miss out on benefits that only private practice offers?

Jaimela (Jami) Dulaney, M.D., cardiologist and owner of a concierge cardiology, internal medicine, and nutrition practice in Port Charlotte, Florida, thinks so.

Dulaney contends that owning a practice offers quality of life that may be impossible to find as an employee. The advantages she cites include more control over her work life and the freedom to pursue clinical passions that don't easily fit into hospital or corporate priorities.

"My father—a business owner, not a physician—gave me advice when I was trying to decide how to manage my career," she says. "He said, 'If somebody has a skill where they can work for themselves, why would they work for anybody else?'" Before launching her one-of-a-kind, plant-based concierge practice in 2017, Dulaney practiced in many settings, including academic medicine, employment and partnership tracks in small and large groups, and a solo cardiology practice.

Many other practice owners agree with Dulaney. Still, neither private practice ownership nor employment is a monolithic option. Within each category, there are opportunities to practice that suit many physician goals. The key is to consider your own personality and aspirations, both short- and long-term, and not to rule anything out based on assumptions that might be incorrect.

The quest for work-life balance

Of all the motivations young physicians express for favoring employment over business ownership, work-life balance may be the most compelling.

Moses Graubard, M.D., an emergency and pain medicine physician with The Permanente Medical Group (TPMG), the physician organization of Kaiser Permanente, in Oakland, California, notes that his job includes features that support physicians in both their work and professional lives. "I believe I work fewer hours than I would in private practice," he says, adding that TPMG's culture has some flexibility built-in. "In addition to clinical practice, our group can offer physicians opportunities that might not be available outside of Kaiser Permanente, such as research and teaching."

He also appreciates that while advancement opportunities are abundant and senior physicians can pursue roles in leadership or administration if they choose, physicians at TPMG who want to focus on patient care can opt to leave virtually all business issues to others.

The idea of "just being a doctor" is a draw for many physicians. But Rosenblum believes younger physicians may not realize how much can be gained, including more work-life balance, by taking on more business responsibility. Much depends on how the practice structures itself: More flexibility can be built into the organization from the start, if that's a priority for practice owners.

"I've noticed younger physicians are very concerned about quality of life and work-life balance, especially because the financial rewards [of being a physician] are less than they once were. These are some of the best and brightest people, and they see that, compared to their friends in finance or software, the economic rewards of medicine aren't as great," he says. "Growing up through 9/11 and the 2008 recession has given them a different sense of the world. They want more security. But they may not realize that private practice may offer more of the balance they're also looking for."

Gregory Harris, D.O., F.A.C.O.I., hematologist/oncologist and practice owner with Harbin Clinic Cancer Center in Rome, Georgia, agrees. "A lot of people like the stability of just knowing 'I show up, I see my set number of patients per week, and I get paid the same.' But they may not realize they're giving up a ton of freedom." Having better work-life balance and more time for family was a key reason he chose to work toward practice ownership right from the start of his career.

Harris says that the key is to "find the right group of likeminded physicians." By design, his group prioritizes flexibility and time off for physicians. "We all work four days. We each have a wellness day every week. We also require four weeks of vacation, but some of us take up to six or seven." It's crucial, he says, to assess culture factors like these before signing on with a group for a partnership or partnership track—or before ruling out private practice altogether in favor of salaried employment.

Kori Hunt, M.D., a family physician with Grants Pass Clinic in Grants Pass, Oregon, remembers interviewing with a partner to join the clinic as an employee a few years ago. She was surprised and impressed when the partner told her, "I've never had to miss one of my daughter's games." About a year after hiring on, Hunt became a partner herself—working part-time, so that she can have more time with her own daughter.

Conventional wisdom may be incorrect

Dulaney was also concerned about work-life balance when raising her child. She was on the partnership track at a large group when she took the uncommon step of opening a solo cardiology practice.

"That's not supposed to work for a cardiologist. How do you survive call?" she recalls. "But I took my own call and worked out an arrangement for a group to cover for me when I went out of town. It was a lot of years of seven-days-a-week call. I was busy, but I made it work."

Most important: by hanging out her shingle, she might have been busier, but she had more freedom.

"As a single mother, I wanted to have some control over my life. [With a solo practice] I could let people know that there were days I'd be coaching track." More recently, she bucked assumptions again when she converted her practice to a concierge model. Patients that share her vision of preventive cardiology care through plant-based nutrition, exercise, and community pay a monthly subscription fee. This has allowed her to reduce her patient panel to about a fifth of what it was in her conventional cardiology practice.

Harris says that oncology is also assumed to be incompatible with private practice, due to high overhead costs and the need to attract referrals. His group operates "like mini-practices under one umbrella," so that overhead costs are shared and the group gains purchasing power. The group's location helps make its business work, too. Referral relationships are fostered because "it's a very medical town," Harris says. Though the community is relatively rural, with population of around 10,000, there are two hospitals, 150 physicians, and 100 nurse practitioners and physician assistants.

After joining her group as a prospective partner, Hunt was delighted when another assumption that had discouraged her from the idea of ownership was debunked.

"Being a partner and business owner didn't cross my mind at first, because I thought I'd have to be involved in all the business details," she says. Her group's partners participate in strategic decisions at a board level. To allow physicians to focus on medicine, the group has dedicated management and clear formulas for partner income and sharing of overhead. Transparency is central to their business philosophy. And each partner also maintains complete control over their schedule.

"I was worried I'd get bogged down in details like billing and hiring and firing," Hunt says. "Our structure allows me to focus on being a doctor, but still have control over my practice."

Clinical decision making and quality of life

Graubard says that generalized assumptions about large organizations related to clinical decision making should be tested by job seekers, as there can be significant differences that affect physician work life.

At TMPG, he says, "our whole organization is run by doctors. Everyone understands what everyone else is dealing with." Because the Kaiser Permanente umbrella comprises TPMG, a hospital organization, and a health plan, he adds, TPMG's physicians don't have to worry about whether a procedure or treatment they recommend will be reimbursed. Not having to deal with insurance hassles may give TPMG's physicians a quality-of-life advantage that's not universally available in employment situations. "We all—the insurance company, the hospitals, and our group—depend on each other for our success," he adds.

Graubard also notes that Kaiser Permanente is not the only organization with this type of set-up. (He mentioned Intermountain and Geisinger, for example, and noted there are probably others.) He says his best advice to job-seeking physicians is to ask questions about the clinical decision-making process in any organization they're considering joining, because it can be so important to career satisfaction. "I urge residents to really use your alumni network from residency. It's so helpful to talk to people who are already working." Sometimes, he points out, you can even learn through networking about an attractive opening in an organization you're targeting before it's even advertised.

Of course, independent clinical decision making can be one of the most appealing aspects of practice ownership. Some private practices, like Dulaney's and Harris's, take clinical decision making in customized directions.

In Dulaney's case, her family history of cardiac problems set her on the path to cardiology—and ignited a passion for prevention. A marathon runner, she focused first on introducing patients to the benefits of exercise. But then books about veganism caught her attention. She wanted to work nutrition into her practice when employed in a large group but found it unworkable.

"I wanted to do a nutrition class and do plant-based cardiology, but the way the group was structured, there was no way to do it and survive. We were caught up in the wheel of seeing a certain number of patients, taking enough call, doing enough hospital work." The message Dulaney received was that she could pursue her ideas for educating patients, but only in her free time. Ultimately, the experience pushed her to develop a new vision for a solo practice with plant-based nutrition as its foundation.

Nutrition was also a keen interest for Harris. He recognized that his rural cancer patients might not have access to nutrition information that could help them be healthier.

"We brought on a full-time nutritionist who could meet with patients while they're in the office getting chemo. In a major company, would I be able to just hire someone like that? They would probably say, 'Why would we do that, when we can't bill for it?'" he says. "In our group, we can decide to just do something like this that can make a huge change for our patients and will cost us very little."

Variety and learning to foster career longevity

The ability to focus on creating protocols and policies that keep patients at the center of care undoubtedly bolsters physician satisfaction. Says Hunt, "We can decide what we feel comfortable with, and what we feel is best and safe for patients and ourselves."

Avoiding burnout is another conscious component of the strategy that guides Harris's practice. He says that in oncology, ensuring that physician morale isn't depleted is essential for patient care.

"Our patient relationships are long-term. We must have good quality of life so that we can be there for them. It comes down to the right set of features," he says, adding that the ideal work situation for one physician might be different from another's. Whether seeking a position in a large organization or joining a private group with the possibility of partnership, Harris urges colleagues to consider these issues of fit very carefully. And if you're planning to partner up with other physicians to start a new group, you have the opportunity to make these decisions about practice life that can make all the difference in your job satisfaction.

Harris adds that he's discovered that he finds improving the operations side of his practice very rewarding. "Patient efficiency is my passion. I don't think patients should have to sit around and wait. I ask, can we improve the lab or check-in and check-out to make them work better?" Tinkering with these workflows inspires him —and is another intellectual outlet that keeps him engaged with his practice. And because he's a practice owner, he can get involved in these issues and try new things without seeking approval from a corporate structure.

Rosenblum also regards the business side of the practice as a form of creative expression—and even fun. "I'm an imperfect business manager, but that's the exciting thing about being in business. There's always a new way to grow it, to tweak things and improve efficiency. It's a way to exercise the non-medical side of my brain."

In Dulaney's case, she'd found the administrative side of practice management in her conventional practice draining. "I felt like I was jumping through all the financial hoops of EMR, meeting payroll, and chasing reimbursement." But when she started to plan her plant-based concierge practice, she found a zest for other business disciplines like strategy and marketing. These newfound interests were ideally suited to promoting both her practice and her message. She has so far recorded more than 200 episodes of her plant-based wellness podcast and has developed classes, written cookbooks, and even partnered with a fine-dining restaurant to offer special vegan selections.

"I've found I enjoy writing all of a sudden," she says. "I see that aspect of my career growing. It has put new life into my practice of medicine."

Graubard adds that a large organization may offer ways to refresh your intellect and your practice, but you might need to seek them out. For example, he was able to take a year's leave from his job to pursue a pain medicine fellowship. This turned out to be not just a stimulating and recharging experience, but an invaluable career step that expanded his practice options.

Do financial concerns supersede all else?

For many residents, the career concern that overwhelms all others is financial.

As Hunt says, "So many physicians graduate with so much debt, it's like you have a mortgage payment without the house. It's understandable that hospitals and other large employers that can offer loan repayment are attractive. Private groups, even large ones, may not be able to compete with that." She points out, though, that your first career step doesn't have to be forever, and that salaried employment is still not a permanent guarantee. She mentions that some colleagues who've shied away from private practice because they're worried about expectations of productivity don't realize that hospitals "are basing compensation on RVUs, too. In some ways, it's like a partnership," but without the financial upside.

Over time, you might also be able to earn more as a private practice physician. The 2019 Medscape Physician Compensation Report, for example, found that self-employed physicians in their survey earned about 24 percent more than employed ones. But a lot depends on your specialty and the market you're working in.

Rosenblum says that California's high cost of living makes employment with a larger system more lucrative for many specialties, at least initially. "They can offer a bigger starting base and a bonus to help buy a home." In some specialties, physicians may also find few private group opportunities when starting out. Opening a small practice typically means delaying some financial rewards, too.

Graubard says, "Here in the East Bay Area, I believe it's estimated that Kaiser Permanente members are about half the insured population." That market dominance makes it more challenging to build a private practice—though not impossible. He says that for some specialties, private groups are more common, and the most successful ones are "rare and coveted opportunities." He adds, though, that this competition, plus the tougher economic environment in California, keeps TPMG focused on providing a work environment and financial benefits that attract the best physicians and encourage them to stay.

Even though some locations, like the Bay Area, may be more financially challenging, Rosenblum advises prioritizing location when starting out. "I think you'll be happiest if you practice in a place where you'll be happy. If you go to a rural place seeking the best economic deal, you have to know what your life will be like beyond medicine." He also points out that while, in other fields, people change jobs or even careers fairly frequently, in medicine, it takes many years (and hard work) to build a reputation and a referral network. These things are especially important to building a private practice, and they matter in employment situations, too.

"I think it's so important to think about location and cultural aspects that are important to your happiness. Money isn't everything," Rosenblum adds.

Planning for the long term

When finances must be prioritized, "working in a hospital may serve an important purpose in the beginning [of a physician career]. But I recommend keeping your eyes open," Hunt says. View that first career step as a learning opportunity—not just to understand more about your profession and your organization, but about your own preferences and priorities. You might find a spot as an employee that suits your personality perfectly—but if not, there are myriad options to explore.

When he was learning about private practice, Harris says he relied on mentors. "I had three very knowledgeable mentors who showed me the books—literally." He adds, though, that mentors can be hard to find. Now that he has the opportunity to give back, he has become one himself. "I talk to residents about the business of medicine and quality of life and work-life balance. I try to get people to start thinking about these things earlier. It's not all about money, but about quality of life and how you want to live it."

Rosenblum says, "This may sound trite, but I still look at the practice of medicine as a privilege and honor. The role you'll play in people's lives is transformative. Finding the environment that is right for you, whether in private practice or employment, is more important than a few extra dollars. Enjoy the process of learning and becoming."

This spirit of being willing to try things—to reach for a happier life—seems to be a common one among private-practice physicians. But being able to take risks requires some planning, too. Avoiding "lifestyle inflation," for example, can provide financial reserves to support trying to build your own practice in the future. And having a Plan B when starting a new venture can make it less risky.

Dulaney says of starting her solo practice, "I knew that if this flunked, I had a back-up plan. I realized I could get part-time work at the ER." She advises to think through how to keep money flowing in if pursuing a passion project takes longer than expected.

"Remember that as a physician," Dulaney adds, "you have the opportunity to do a whole host of things. In the practice of medicine, and the practice of life, you hone what's right for you as you go along."

Rosenblum echoes the sentiment. "A lot is gained in life by not necessarily doing what the herd is doing. I'd like to tell residents that, in my opinion, private practice is certainly not dead."

A shorter version of this chapter appeared as a feature article in PracticeLink magazine's Winter 2021 issue.

CHAPTER 9: FINDING YOUR FIT: FIVE QUESTIONS YOU'RE NOT ASKING

Marlene Grenon, M.D., CM, associate professor of surgery at University of California-San Francisco and adjunct professor at the International Space University, Strasbourg, France, has known since she was a teenager that she wanted to pursue aerospace medicine. Having such a clear vision gave her a leg up in planning her career—if only because it narrowed her options. But even when you're committed to a specific niche of medicine, Grenon notes, there are still many choices to make that affect everything from your ability to avoid burnout, to having a satisfying balance of work life and family life, to keeping your options open down the road.

"Listening to your gut is so important," Grenon tells her mentees at UCSF. "The environment that you work in, the team that you work with, it's so important. You need to find the right fit."

Your gut can help you find the environment that will make your first—or next—work experience satisfying and rewarding. But to engage your instincts to help you choose well, it's important to first ask the right questions. That means not just doing a thorough job of quizzing your would-be employers. You need to ask *yourself* some big questions, too. Here are five important ones you may not have considered. These can help you tackle important career decisions with confidence, whether you're contemplating a specific job or just trying to decide on a practice setting.

Have I built the right network?

A strong, diverse personal network is an invaluable asset to career decision making. One key reason: not all jobs are posted, and your ideal fit may be more likely to come through a friend or other trusted contact, especially one you've worked with before.

Azra Ashraf, M.D., MPH, a plastic surgeon in private practice in Washington, DC, recently found a new job through a friend she met in residency, leaving behind a role that wasn't a good fit. She believes working with contemporaries leads to a natural rapport that fosters a positive work experience. "Now I'll work alongside friends whose personalities I already know, and whose values I know I share."

Even though networking is so valuable to career planning, many new physicians are unaware of its power. After all, it's not something physicians are taught in medical school or residency, where the focus is almost entirely on academic credentials.

"Too many young physicians think that if I tick the right boxes, if I go to the right medical school and do the right residency, that's enough" to set them on their way, says Andrew Cain McClary, M.D., staff physician with Grand Rounds and consulting assistant professor of pathology at Stanford University. But mentors and connections won't materialize without effort, he says. "Success is about the hustle, too."

Josh Parker, M.D., a pediatrician with Pediatric Wellness Group, Inc., in Redwood City, California, adds that advisers from outside your immediate circle provide essential perspective in evaluating your career options. "Without help from people with business knowledge or more experience in medicine, it's hard to even know what questions to ask potential employers." Understanding the implications of contract terms, for example, is easier with help from others with relevant experience.

Networking can feel awkward to young professionals in any field, and physicians are no exception. But you don't have to look too far to establish—or reestablish—a diverse network. Connections like family members and your undergraduate classmates can be invaluable.

"My undergraduate friends kept me connected to the business world, helping me learn where investors see opportunities in medicine," McClary says. With help from his peers, he began to see an intersection of technology and the "old-school" slide analysis process of pathology. This led him to think about a move to Silicon Valley to explore start-up opportunities driven by the Sand Hill Road venture capital community.

Another low-stress way to expand your network is simply to lend a hand, whether by filling a volunteer opportunity or providing advice, feedback, or a personal introduction to a peer in need. "If you can do something for someone, that's a favor in the bank," McClary observes. Don't forget, he reminds, to be ready to return the favors of people who help you along the way.

If you're starting out in a market near your residency or fellowship, those connections can also be valuable—sometimes in unexpected ways. Josh Parker found himself presented with a career opportunity that was nearly ideal, except that it wasn't full time. He turned to his residency connections for ideas, and that led to a part-time role caring for high-risk babies in two local hospitals— something he hadn't previously considered, but that filled his open time and evolved into a passion.

Am I limiting my options unnecessarily?

When large student loan balances loom, many young physicians respond by limiting themselves to opportunities that appear to offer the most secure compensation. But after working in a role that wasn't a match for her goals or work style, Azra Ashraf now sees value in being more open-minded about practice settings and compensation models. In her new position, her income will be 100 percent based on the revenue she generates—and she is confident she'll be happier.

"Our structure is solo practices with cost-sharing. I'll have the autonomy to pave my own way," she says. The structure gives her the freedom to make decisions about what marketing to do or whether to add staff or a physician assistant, since these costs would come out of her own revenue stream.

Financially, it may seem risky—but promises of guaranteed income in more "typical" employment situations may not be realistic either, especially if they're based on aggressive, best-case productivity goals. "What I've learned is that if it looks too good financially, it probably isn't realistic," adds Ashraf.

McClary also believes it's important to be open-minded—even when considering your first job, and even when loans are a concern. "The financial burden is ridiculous, but you can't lose sight of how needed we are." If your skills are indispensable, a company might even help with the loan burden.

Rather than fighting disruptive economic trends, McClary suggests that young physicians consider applying their training to new medical and business models. Start-up ventures that seek to transform the way health care is delivered—like the one McClary works for—are scooping up young physicians and expanding their options for contributing to medicine.

"The skill set you gain in medicine is so valuable. You can apply that knowledge in many settings," adds Marlene Grenon. She notes that even for physicians who start out in a typical practice setting, there are many opportunities to switch to, say, a pharma company or a health-care start-up down the road. "You can apply your knowledge to a completely different area."

Do I know what's really needed to be successful?

The first career step after training inevitably comes with expectations, both written and unwritten. It's not uncommon for a new physician to find that "learning the ropes" comes with surprises—and sometimes frustration if the rules for success aren't clear.

"When you're a new doctor in a large organization, your superiors will notice if, say, you're ordering a blood test for every kid with a cough and a runny nose," Josh Parker says. "It's appropriate for them to question, but it's also normal to need to learn these things" when you're in your first job.

Parker advises asking prospective employers how you'll get input and advice from more experienced colleagues—and what the culture dictates about asking for help. Is it OK to just knock on a colleague's door? Or is there a more formal process for gaining needed everyday skills? Specific questions like these can help you prepare for the norms of your new organization. The answers can give you a clearer sense of the culture as well.

"Before accepting a position, be sure you know what you'll be evaluated on, the way feedback is delivered, and how you'll get help to improve," Parker adds.

Productivity goals are common in physician contracts, and it's important to understand what will be necessary to meet them. Asking about the number of patients you'll need to see each day to meet revenue goals will help you clarify expectations—but your ability to keep pace is just one piece of the productivity puzzle.

You'll also need to be sure that enough patients are available for you to see.

When Azra Ashraf was asked to expand her practice's business in a new area, she found that a hotly competitive market and other barriers that were not immediately obvious made the task more difficult than she expected.

"One challenge was that it was hard to attract referrals because we accepted only a handful of insurance plans," she explains. "Primary care physicians want to refer to surgeons that meet their patients' preferences," and most patients place the ability to use their insurance at the top of the list.

When compensation is tied to revenue goals, it's always a good idea to be sure you'll be able to accept the health plans that are most popular among your target patients. And if the practice doesn't have enough overflow demand already to keep you busy, you'll also need to know what help you'll get to attract more patients. For example, have important marketing channels such as hospital relationships and online marketing been established?

Other aspects of the practice infrastructure—such as EHR and other technologies in place, and support staff per physician—also contribute significantly to physicians' ability to be fully productive. If possible, it's helpful to meet the staff who'll support you, to gauge your ability to communicate and the staff's commitment to growing your practice. Benchmarking data from organizations like the Medical Group Management Association (MGMA) is another excellent tool to help you infer how well a potential employer supports its physicians with staffing compared with its peers, as well as its comparative financial performance.

How can I stay creative and engaged?

The pace of change in health care and increasing demands placed on physicians make burnout much more of a factor than ever before. It's not too early to think about how you'll stay challenged, motivated, and committed to medicine even when considering your very first position.

"In medical school, you're learning all these facts," says McClary. "If all you're going to do at work is repeat those facts, you're going to burn out. Burnout is real."

"We're all searching to make a difference in the world and help others," Grenon adds. A mix of activities—from practicing, to teaching, to performing research—helps Grenon stay engaged and exercise her creativity. "When we're doing research, we're at the edge of science, and we have to think of new concepts. We have to be creative to find better ways to solve problems."

While Grenon believes her academic post helps her find opportunities to stretch her intellectual muscles, physicians in large health systems and private practices can find opportunities to keep growing and contribute in new ways, even if they have to look a little harder. Clinical research pairs well with private practice, for example.

Other physicians look to give back through volunteer opportunities, at home or internationally. Azra Ashraf is committed to an annual trip to Pakistan, where she works with a British colleague to treat victims of domestic violence. The flexibility to commit time to this volunteer work was another factor that weighed heavily in choosing her current position.

"You become unidimensional in medical school," Ashraf says. "When you start your career, it's your chance to go back to your original vision, to what led you to seek your degree." Besides her volunteer commitment, for Ashraf, getting back to her original vision meant reconnecting with her interest in public policy, which led her to pursue an MPH during medical school and also influenced her choice of a new practice located in Washington, D.C.

McClary adds that it's important to remember that it's more possible than ever to pursue multiple tracks in parallel, and that variety keeps your career fresh. "Our training involves a rigid system. But your career can be flexible—there's pharma, outpatient work, digital health. You can freelance and participate in several options."

How does this organization fit into my long-term vision? And do I fit into theirs?

When you're considering options for your very first job after a lengthy academic journey, your long-term career might be the last thing on your mind. But even if many of your goals and plans are yet to be determined, it's useful to try to pin down some of your priorities—if only to avoid unpleasant surprises or feeling "stuck."

"Don't forget to consider what happens when the contract ends," advises Josh Parker. If a contract you're evaluating doesn't specifically discuss renewal or extension, you may not be able to stay on with the practice at the end of your term. That can be a problem if the contract also includes restrictive covenants that don't permit you to join another organization in the same area—especially if you've invested a lot of time and energy creating a patient panel you're no longer allowed to serve.

Building up a practice in one spot can also make it financially unattractive to start over in another community later on, which can be a big challenge if you had your heart set on settling down and starting a family somewhere else.

"I recommend thinking about where you want to live, and trying to find a position there, keeping in mind that there has to be enough demand for your specialty in the area," says Azra Ashraf. Contracts that include financial perks that have to be earned out, such as loan repayments or relocation expenses tied to the contract term or revenue goals, can also make moving costly if your plans change before the terms are met.

Location may also be a factor if you're hoping to switch at some point from a traditional practice environment to a pharmaceutical or device vendor, or a biotech or health IT start-up. And it pays to do some research before deciding where you'll land, since your options extend beyond the best-known venture capital hubs of the Silicon Valley, Boston, New York, and Los Angeles. Energy (and capital) for pharmaceutical research, biotechnology ventures, and other types of healthcare start-ups has coalesced in the last decade in places like Tampa, San Diego, Austin, Houston, Nashville, and the Research Triangle area of North Carolina.

And what if the job you're considering is the one you hope to stick with for the long haul? It's important to get as close a read as you can on the practice's own five- or ten-year plan. For example, if you're joining a small, private practice and believe you'll prefer that type of environment, try to assess the practice's commitment to staying independent.

"Smaller practices often end up selling and joining up with larger groups because a senior partner decides to retire, and none of the other partners wants to deal with managing," Parker points out.

If you believe you'll want to be a partner yourself someday, try to understand the motivations and priorities of the current partners —as well as what it would take to join them down the road. For example, would you need to buy in to become a partner? And should you think about management training along the way?

Regardless of how sure you are that the setting attracting you today is the best one for you in the long term, you may find that it's a perfect fit once you've started—so be as clear as you can be on whether the organization plans to keep moving in the same direction in years to come.

Your first step in a long career—with many potential paths

A common theme shared by Drs. Ashraf, Grenon, McClary, and Parker is the benefit of remaining open to a wide variety of possibilities. After so many years of studying and preparing, it's natural to want to make the best possible choice in your first role on your own as a physician. But remember that your vision of an ideal career may change as you progress.

In many ways, there's never been a better time to be a physician. Opportunities abound in many settings. Wherever you land today, you'll learn something to help you in your next role. The key at every stage is to be open to—and invest time in thinking about—your many potential options.

A shorter version of this chapter appeared as a feature in PracticeLink magazine's Spring 2016 issue.

CHAPTER 10: WHY—AND HOW—TO INVOLVE YOUR SPOUSE IN YOUR JOB SEARCH

If the end of your training is finally in sight and you're eyeing the brass ring of your first job as a practicing physician, the search process may feel like one more test for you to ace—the next phase of a years-long gauntlet that began with pre-med studies and your MCATs. Given your track record of competently tackling every challenge on your own, you might assume you should do the same with your career planning. But if you're married or in a long-term relationship, you're likely making a mistake if you go it alone.

For one thing, your life partner can help you manage the array of time-consuming new tasks that come with the job-search process. But much more important than that, your spouse can help you make a better decision for you and your family—and potentially avoid one you'll regret.

What's behind first-job turnover?

Studies show that as many as half of residents don't stick with their first jobs beyond a few years. Though the possible reasons are many, it seems clear that residents as a group are not, on average, choosing jobs that suit them for the long haul.

Shane Halvorsen is a business consultant, spouse of a physician, and past president and board member of Advocates for the American Osteopathic Association (AAOA), an advocacy arm of the national association for D.O.s. One of AAOA's goals is to create community among families of D.O.s. AAOA's membership includes spouses of physicians at all stages of their careers.

Based on his conversations with AAOA members, Halvorsen believes that, in at least some cases, first-job turnover could be caused by a failure to fully consider the whole family's needs when choosing among offers. He adds, though, that even during his relatively recent experience as the physician spouse, he's noticed medicine is changing—and both physicians and employers are increasingly aware of the need to include spouses and family priorities in job decisions.

Halvorsen's spouse, Vanessa Halvorsen, D.O., is currently completing her otolaryngology residency at Freeman Hospital in Joplin, Missouri, and preparing for one more year of training, a fellowship in rhinology and skull base surgery. She's already receiving and considering solicitations from recruiters. Vanessa and Shane work together to analyze the priorities and trade-offs they'll consider when she decides on a position next year.

Among the Halvorsens' main concerns is location, which will affect Shane's potential consulting income. Shane and Vanessa also want to be sure that their new community has the resources and amenities they need for their growing family.

Shane Halvorsen says that with every opportunity Vanessa is presented, "We always sit down and talk about it and go through it first together. Before she'll [accept an] interview, we ask ourselves, 'Could this actually work for me as well?'"

While his wife will likely earn a significantly higher salary, he says that's not the only consideration, and that finding a location that works for both of their careers is a goal.

"She's invested all this time, energy, and money into her career," Shane Halvorsen says. "But I've also invested in mine."

Vanessa Halvorsen adds that while career prospects for both partners are a top concern in her family's case, spouses who aren't working outside the home also need to be involved in evaluating relocation options. She recalls that one of the interns in her residency program is married with four children, with three of them already in school. His spouse's top priority was to stay close to the community where he'd been training, to keep the kids in their current school system and maintain her community connections.

"She's been building her family's structure of support while her husband has been in medical school and residency. I think it's important that he's honored that and made their current location his number one choice," Dr. Halvorsen says.

Liz Mahan, director of professional development and solutions with the Association for Advancing Physician and Provider Recruitment, adds that in her experience as a physician recruiter, she has often met candidates who were searching for a new position because the location of their current one didn't work for their spouses. Often, she says, it's been the spouse who researched and found the opportunity at her health care system.

"When we got into why they were looking, the answer always was, 'my partner or my spouse is not happy where we are and I work crazy-long hours,'" she recalls.

Mahan adds that it's not unusual for physicians to say it doesn't matter to them where they live—they just want to practice. If that's you, it's a good idea to put your spouse's location preferences at the top of the list, since they will likely have many reasons for preferring one location over another. And if you don't think through those reasons and wind up in a spot that doesn't suit them, they'll be struggling on their own in a place they don't like while you're working long hours in your new practice.

"There's a lot of alone time for your spouse, not just while you're training, but even while you're working," adds Napoleon Bonaparte Higgins, M.D., a psychiatrist in the Houston area and author of *Transition 2 Practice: 21 Things Every Doctor Must Know in Contract Negotiations and the Job Search*. "You may actually be working more as an attending than you did as a resident. So now your spouse is in a city where they may not want to be, or where they may not know many people, facing a lot of time alone."

"I've unfortunately seen physicians over the years who ended up leaving our practice for the sole reason that their spouse wasn't happy in our rural area of East Texas," says Jenni Holman, M.D., FAAD, dermatologist and regional president, East & South Texas, with U.S. Dermatology Partners.

Holman adds that it's important to remember that choosing a location that suits your spouse and family supports your well-being, too.

"Our residency training teaches us to ignore our emotional and personal needs as a sign of strength at work. When we enter the real world, often we continue to lack the skills needed for life balance to prevent burnout," Holman says. "Clearly, having a spouse at home who is happy and in agreement with where you've chosen to build a life is key to the ability to recharge at home."

Spousal support: Inventorying family needs

Creating a complete list of needs and considerations for choosing your new job may seem like a daunting task, but that's just one more reason to involve your spouse in the process. Encouraging your partner to participate in—or even take charge of—this part of your search can both ensure that his or her voice is heard and make the workload more manageable.

Hashing out priorities and possible compromises in advance will also ultimately be more efficient: By ruling out opportunities that don't tick the needed boxes, you'll avoid wasting time and effort on unnecessary interviews and site visits.

Location is usually the most important consideration, so it makes sense to start by building a list of possibilities and ruling out non-starters, says Peter Moskowitz, M.D., executive director of the Center for Professional and Personal Renewal in Palo Alto, California, which offers physician coaching, and clinical professor of radiology, emeritus, at the Stanford University School of Medicine.

"Regardless of how exciting the first new job may be, the life portion of work-life balance is still important. The culture of the community, the geographic location, the weather, the opportunity to do things that are fun and so forth all also matter. If you have a spouse and you're involving them in the process, they can help you evaluate all these things," Moskowitz says.

Moskowitz points out that it can be helpful for spouses to take the lead on evaluating cities you're both unfamiliar with. One way to start is by contacting alumni of the spouse's college who live in the community you're considering. That way, you both can get reliable input about everything from macro issues like the political climate and school quality to daily life amenities like gyms, restaurants, and shopping.

Two-career families: Getting the calculus right

Besides quality-of-life issues, relocation may have a significant impact on a spouse's or partner's career. In some cases, a move could affect your spouse's compensation, or even make it impossible for them to continue in the same line of work. A self-employed spouse might find they can work anywhere—or they might find that a move means they'll be starting their business over from scratch.

Since your partner is in the best position to evaluate the impact of a move on their career, the earlier they start to research prospective communities and analyze the full financial upside and downside, the better.

Mark Fleischman, M.D., a dermatologist, fellowship-trained Mohs surgeon, and Midwest regional president of U.S. Dermatology Partners in the Kansas City metro area, points out that it's not unusual for physicians to be married to other health care professionals. In those cases, the spouse might find employment in the same organization as their physician partner, and the non-physician's compensation could stay roughly the same (or at least be easily projected).

But when the spouse works in a different field, the availability of similar job opportunities will likely be an important factor in whether the community will work for the family—and pay scales aren't the only consideration.

"A lot of times there won't be family nearby in the new community," Fleischman says. "If the physician and their spouse have children, they'll have to be sure there are opportunities for quality childcare and education." The costs of childcare and education will also need to be factored into the equation.

Higgins adds that while it may seem obvious that the physician's career opportunities should take priority simply because the compensation will likely be so much higher, it's critical to test that assumption thoroughly.

For example, what if your spouse is employed in a job that earns a pension, and that pension is only five, ten, or even fifteen years away? Your household could miss out on a huge source of income if your partner leaves that job prematurely, even if the physician salary is much higher.

"That could be a $3,000 or $4,000 monthly check that your spouse would receive until death," he says—pension payments that could amount to many hundreds of thousands of dollars you could share. "That could be twenty years or more of income you didn't even have to work for."

With accumulated experience and expertise, your spouse also might be positioned to level up over the coming years if they stay the course. This makes it all the more important to try to project the true cost of starting fresh in another city—especially if their work involves building a clientèle over time—for instance, as an attorney or CPA. And if your spouse works in a corporate environment with the opportunity to invest in a retirement plan with a matched contribution, or if life insurance is part of the benefits package, that should be accounted for as well.

Besides your partner's potential to contribute an increasing proportion of your family's income over time, Higgins says, their career progress provides another advantage that could be priceless: flexibility.

"With physician finances, one of the biggest things that gives you options is when you don't have risk," he says, noting that the most common and burdensome financial risk for physicians is medical school debt. "If you have a high-earning spouse, that decreases your risk."

With less risk comes financial flexibility that could enable you to try something different—even a non-clinical job—in the future. Just knowing you have this option to try something new, if someday you want to, can stave off the sense of being "trapped" in a clinical grind that contributes to burnout.

Moskowitz adds that "even in dual-physician families, there can be an assumption that the highest paid doctor's career should come first. That can become problematic for the relationship if both physicians decide they want to make a change, or if their top job choices are in different cities." When he coaches such couples, he suggests they work out 'sequential transitions'—meaning that one partner gets the practice situation of their choice for a time period, then the other gets their turn.

"When both partners are physicians," he says, "career change for one almost always means an involuntary change for the other. The [implied] question is always, 'whose career happiness is more important?'"

The negotiated trading off of career changes is not ideal, since it means more disruption and effort. But Moskowitz says "it's perceived by dual-physician couples to be equitable and fair, which is ultimately much more important."

Higgins adds that while money is important and can seem like a straightforward way to compare opportunities for your family, it may not be the best or only way.

"You may be thinking, 'I'm going to be making $310,000 a year, and my partner only makes $48,000, so they should find another nonprofit to work at. But if that individual feels like they're really doing the work that they need to do, and they love the work and it's making a huge impact, then money may not always be the only consideration."

"You can be a doctor almost anywhere," he observes, but the job your spouse loves at, say, a church or a local nonprofit may not be easily replaceable.

Sharing the job-search administrative workload

As you think through what you want out of your first job, you'll also likely face a lot of new administrative work: research, correspondence, and writing and editing tasks. Many of these are things your spouse can help with.

For example, your cover letters, and potentially even your CV, should be customized to show genuine interest in your preferred employment prospects. If your spouse has worked in the corporate world, he or she may have helpful experience creating these kinds of personal marketing documents. And an extra set of eyes for proofreading your CV and cover letters is always a good idea.

Though many employers will likely reach out to you, you probably won't want to limit your search to those that find you through your residency or fellowship. To expand your flow of leads, your spouse can help with setting up your profiles on LinkedIn and on job boards like PracticeLink. Once you've identified some communities and practice settings to target, your spouse can also help with researching opportunities that may not be posted on job boards—and tracking down contact information.

Since you'll both be interested in reviewing emails as they arrive, consider setting up a job-search email address that you can both monitor. Using a different address from your primary one also helps prevent your regular inbox from becoming overloaded with additional job-related messages.

Site visits: Divide and conquer

Once you reach the site-visit stage, be sure the organization you're considering joining permits—and, ideally, encourages—your spouse to come along.

"When physicians who are married interview in our practice, we try to be sure a dinner includes our physicians' spouses (and kids if the candidate's kids are visiting) as well," Holman says. "Candidate spouses' conversations with our physicians' spouses can reveal insights on lifestyle and the job opportunity."

Moskowitz adds, "I've had coaching clients pursuing new jobs and savvy physician groups and departments have lined up the spouse with a real estate broker to visit neighborhoods, networking with community leaders, and introductions to local people in the spouse's industry, all while the M.D. is consumed with interviews related to the potential new job."

Mahan agrees. She says that in-house recruiters increasingly engage in separate efforts to meet the needs of spouses and families. Besides realtors and job-related contacts, recruiters can help spouses and physician candidates learn about schools, local amenities, and all manner of activities the family is interested in—so don't hesitate to ask a recruiter for help.

"Recruiters are exceptional networkers," she says. "And we're 'people people.' If you have a consideration or your spouse does, we're more than happy to connect you with people who can give you a full picture of what your life would be like."

With the help of the in-house recruiter, administrator, or physician leader who is bringing you on site, your spouse can—and should—schedule as many information-gathering tasks as he or she wants to help with your mutual decision. Be sure to relay to the recruiter anything that is important to you or your spouse—no matter how tangential your questions may seem.

"It doesn't hurt to ask, even if you think it sounds a little wacky," Mahan says. She recalls one physician she recruited whose wife was not concerned about their relocation from a job perspective, since her consulting job could be done remotely. However, the physician did eventually reveal two things of intense interest to his wife: she had horses and she loved yoga. As it turned out, Mahan was uniquely able to help his spouse out with information about local horse-boarding options and yoga studios, since Mahan herself is a horse owner and is also a big fan of yoga.

Who knows you better?

While you're on site for your interview, your spouse can also provide an extra perspective on the opportunity you're considering. He or she could spot potential issues that you might overlook while you're focusing on selling yourself.

"A spouse can be the sounding board for what's really going to make you happy in your career and what's going to make you happy in a new community," says Robyn Alley-Hay, M.D., an OB/GYN physician and physician coach in Dallas. Alley-Hay says that because your spouse knows you so well, they can help make sure you're considering all the possibilities, including some that are "outside the box" of typical jobs.

Holman agrees. "Oftentimes when a physician, especially a new career physician, is focused on impressing the interviewer and presenting their best self, they don't play the cynic or look for what may be different than what is promised," she says. Spouses can look for negative signs or question marks, she adds, freeing their physician partner to concentrate on their interview performance.

"In a marriage, people are typically wired differently. Having a different perspective on the practice, the opportunity, and the people is helpful. Typically, the physician is focused on the job. The spouse can be focused on how the opportunity impacts their marriage and family and ask those questions as well."

Contributing special expertise

Even if they don't have legal or contract administration expertise, your spouse's fresh-eyed look at offers you're considering will help you understand the details and how they will affect your family, says Alley-Hay. But if your spouse has applicable career expertise, that "in-house talent" can be even more beneficial—so don't hesitate to tap it.

For example, if your partner works in healthcare administration, he or she might have a detailed set of questions you should ask related to productivity pay. A spouse who's a lawyer could help with the legalese of offers and contracts. Human resources experience, or virtually any kind of corporate experience, could also be helpful in evaluating salary and benefits.

Mahan encourages physicians to ask the recruiter if they can involve their spouse in relevant discussions. "When meeting one-on-one, I found some physicians would say, 'It's my husband that knows all about insurance. Can he come in here so he can ask questions?'" She says this is usually perfectly appropriate but acknowledges that there are some instances when the organization must deal with the candidate directly and alone.

"With the financials, you want to negotiate with the candidate because there are legal implications," she points out, since it will be the physician who signs the contract.

It's also worth noting that in a private practice setting, especially, too much *direct* involvement of a spouse in negotiations—such as an attorney spouse attempting to act as an intermediary, or a practice manager or CFO getting too involved in assessing the business —can be considered a red flag. It may cause the practice partners to fear the spouse will interfere in decision making down the road.

Facilitating your partner's involvement

If you've got a busy partner who's already over-scheduled with career and family obligations, you might assume they won't want to be involved in your job search. If you behave as if that's the case, your spouse may simply go with the flow, rather than insert themselves into your job-search process, given that he or she already has too much to do. But the best advice is probably not to let that happen. Instead, try to find ways to involve them without adding any more stress than necessary.

For example, you can take the lead on asking recruiters for the kinds of community information that can be gleaned on your site visits (which your spouse should still plan to attend). If your spouse hasn't yet come up with a list of concerns, the recruiter can make suggestions and arrange for your partner to meet other physician spouses while on-site or reach out to them afterward.

Remember, too, that your recruiter might hesitate to ask you about your spouse or family, since those sorts of questions could come across as intrusive or discriminatory. That's another reason it's important that you, as the candidate, let the recruiter know how they can help you and your spouse.

Alley-Hay says, "I think it helps to have your recruiter know more about you." Unless you share concerns with the recruiter, they might not bring up things like on-boarding for spouses and families, she adds. It's up to you, as the candidate, to ask.

Support each other

Job hunting, while exciting, is also stressful, says Alley-Hay. Throw a relocation into the mix and your family is now involved in two of life's most stressful transitions at the same time.

With communication and consideration, you and your spouse can help each other get through what could be a taxing process together.

"You know, it's not a bad time, it's just a really difficult one—or it can be," she says. "Any time we go into transition, there's stress. So having that in mind and being very understanding of each other, possibly talking about, 'let's be more understanding of each other right now,' can help alleviate stress."

Moskowitz suggests that keeping regular family routines on track should be a priority. Your spouse may be able to help with that, or you can work on it together. For example, kids' activities ideally shouldn't be interrupted because of the job search.

"Schedule family fun," he says, cautioning that "children's needs can get lost while you and your spouse are hashing out compromises until the wee hours every night."

Above all, keep in mind why you and your spouse are together in the first place.

"Most doctors will say that their spouse is their best friend. But if they are your best friend, then you want to treat them with respect and love. And the way you do that is by communicating, being transparent, and making win-win decisions," Moskowitz adds.

A shorter version of this chapter appeared as a feature in PracticeLink magazine's Spring 2023 issue.

PART FOUR:
INTERVIEWING AND
DECISION MAKING

CHAPTER 11: FIVE RED FLAGS FOR RECRUITERS—AND HOW TO TURN THEM GREEN

With demand for M.D.s and D.O.s in most specialties strong in much of the country, you might think physicians could do no wrong in the job-search process. But recruiters still find mistakes, issues, and omissions in physician job applications that they regard as red flags—information that raises questions and may make a recruiter hesitant to proceed with your application. If you're unaware of these red flags or don't take steps to address them, they could cost you a shot at the job you most want.

Fortunately, there are straightforward ways to turn almost any red flag green. Here are five of the most common application issues that give recruiters pause, and what you can do about them.

Unexplained gaps in training or employment

One red flag for nearly every recruiter: gaps in your curriculum vitae (CV).

A gap is simply an unaccounted-for period in the chronology of your employment or training history, such as when there is a long break between two jobs, or when your training took longer than expected or seems to be missing a block of time.

"Big gaps are a red flag for me—especially post-fellowship gaps," says Cathleen Biga, M.S.N., FACC, president/CEO of Cardiovascular Management of Illinois, member of the board of trustees of the American College of Cardiology, and chair of the board of managers of MedAxiom.

Biga is quick to add, though, that such post-training gaps are less unusual today than in the past, since some young physicians opt to take a break or travel the world before starting their first post-training jobs. "But here's the problem," she says. "They won't even have a chance to meet with me [if the reason for the gap is not explained]."

Recruiters are trained to notice gaps in training and employment, according to Liz Mahan, physician recruitment advisor with the Association for Advancing Physician and Provider Recruitment. "But sometimes those gaps are red flags, and sometimes they're red herrings."

For example, Mahan says, when physicians switch jobs or relocate, credentialing or licensing can take many months—leaving a hole in the candidate's work history that couldn't have been helped. In situations like this, the recruiter's internal alarm bell can easily be silenced with a short, explanatory statement on the CV or in a cover letter.

Linda Cindric, MSOL, CMSR, lead provider recruiter of Geisinger in Danville, Pennsylvania, agrees, and encourages applicants to head off recruiter hesitancy before it happens.

"We like to see gaps addressed on the CV," she says. If the reason for the gap is something you're uncomfortable putting in writing, she adds, "at a minimum, be ready to talk about it during your phone screening. But I encourage addressing it on the CV [if possible], because you don't want to be passed over just because of gaps."

While a short phrase on the CV is an efficient way to address a gap when the explanation is clear-cut, Cindric says that sharing the reason in a cover letter is another option. That approach provides more space if you're prepared to include details about a potentially confusing part of your CV.

But keep in mind that in some instances—such as a medical or personal leave—it's appropriate to be cautious about sharing private details on any document that could be circulated widely.

Mahan adds that you shouldn't worry you'll be expected to discuss a confidential matter like a medical or personal leave in depth. With sensitive situations, she suggests that a short phrase noting the type of leave in general terms could help keep the door open for you to have an interview—and then, if the matter is personal, you should explain it as such. "A recruiter is not going to ask for details [of these situations]. Recruiters really just want to know that you left an opportunity in good standing, and that you still have a license and can be credentialed to practice in a new organization."

Whether the gap is in your employment history or your training, not addressing it could relegate your CV to the "maybe" or even the "reject" folder. Mahan says that's because when gaps are completely unacknowledged in your CV and cover letter, "a recruiter will wonder if you left without a plan—or were asked to leave and so had no opportunity to plan."

The impact of a gap on your CV may partly depend on the job you're applying for or the location you're targeting. If you're aiming for a highly competitive position, not addressing a gap at your earliest opportunity is more likely to limit your chances.

"If you're job seeking for a smaller market with greater unmet demand in your specialty, you may not need to explain the gap in your cover letter or in the CV itself," Biga says. But if you're applying for highly competitive spots in organizations like the Cleveland Clinic or major cities like LA or New York, it's better to take steps to ensure questions raised by your CV don't derail your candidacy before it starts.

"For Chicago, for instance, I just needed to hire five physicians in the last two months," Biga adds. "All of them were my first choices—I called, interviewed them, hired them." She says that for that popular location, the CVs with unexplained gaps or other surface issues never made it out of her "hold" folder for further consideration.

Above all, Biga says, it's always best to be truthful and proactive.

"I had a candidate with a weird gap. It turned out that their background check wasn't going to bear out. [But] they were very up-front about the situation, and we ended up hiring them."

The take-away, Biga says, is to be honest—and get out ahead of the issue. "If something's going to come up, do not wait for it to come up and expect me to call you [to ask about it]."

Bottom line: Though some issues with employment or training history may seem insurmountable, being honest and up-front offers a better chance of overcoming them than hoping a recruiter will look past them.

Jumping from job to job—or fellowship to fellowship

Another red flag recruiters notice is "job jumping"—a recruiter's shorthand for changing employers frequently.

Job jumping is a red flag because it suggests you won't stick with a position for at least a few years if hired. Switching fellowships or residency programs in mid-stream can create the same impression. Recruiters care about these signals because even experienced physicians face a significant ramp-up period to full productivity in a new setting. And for candidates coming straight out of training, it might take several years before a physician contributes profitably to the organization.

Just like employment and training gaps, though, there are often perfectly reasonable explanations for switches. Explaining the reasons up-front can reduce your chances of being tripped up by incorrect assumptions.

With respect to training, Biga notes that otherwise strong candidates are sometimes affected by short space in desirable programs and may need to switch to a different type of fellowship or seek further training offshore. In other cases, physicians may switch because their residency program lost its accreditation. Or in some instances, residents or fellows simply decide a different specialty would be a better fit, and so make a change before they miss the opportunity to do so.

Once clarified, these types of situations would rarely be deal-breakers, Biga says. But it's important to explain the situation, to make sure your CV isn't filtered out before you're even considered.

Once employed, some physicians find they need fresh challenges to thrive at work, Mahan adds. This can lead to job jumping, which in turn can make finding the next position more difficult.

Mahan emphasizes that a need for variety and new challenges is not something to hide or feel bad about—"it's part of what makes you *you*"—but because it can trigger serious recruiter concerns, it is something to manage in both your job search and your career, even if you're just starting out.

"It's a bit of a risky hire if it seems someone is going to leave [soon after joining]," she says. While organizations differ in their tolerance for that risk, she adds, for many employers, frequent job changes are the biggest red flag they worry about.

"Your first question as a recruiter is, 'Why isn't this person staying in a job?' Sometimes, it's just the nature of the person."

If this is you, Mahan says, there are better ways to find the variety you need than changing employers. She remembers a physician she once worked with who "had no grass growing under his feet." He had an unquenchable thirst for new challenges but didn't solve the problem by looking for a new job. Instead, he satisfied that need for novelty by seeking out new "pet projects" within the organization. He found ways to stay engaged without leaving the hospital—a win-win.

It might seem counter-intuitive to let your boss know you're getting bored in your job or try to seek out new challenges inside your hospital or practice, but "most employers would rather keep you than have you leave," both for productivity reasons and to preserve continuity of care for patients, Mahan emphasizes. "If you're contemplating leaving, have that conversation before you do. I would wager a guess that most organizations would rather work with a physician to challenge them and keep them satisfied than look for someone to replace them."

And if you're a physician seeking your first post-training job and you already know you like variety and change, know that your desire to take on new and different challenges could be an asset to the right employer. The key is knowing yourself and your needs before interviewing for a position, and then asking the right questions in the interview process. For example, if you're applying for a role in an academic hospital, you could ask what research or teaching opportunities exist and how you'd pursue those options down the road. Or if the job is with a community hospital, you could ask about leadership opportunities, or the prospect of developing new programs in the future, or ways of getting involved in community outreach.

What if you've been out of training for a while, are on a job search, and are concerned because you've already had a few job jumps?

Short job tenure "is probably something that's better handled in a cover letter than on your CV," Mahan says, especially if you've learned that you need variety but are committed to finding it in place in your next job. If the reason for an untimely job switch is something straightforward and unlikely to recur, though (say, you moved to be closer to a family member who needed help, or because of a spouse's job change), a simple statement on the CV can help you avoid being screened out of the process.

"It's really about getting to that initial phone call," Mahan adds.

Insufficient interview preparation

The process of polishing your CV and identifying the locations and organizations you want to apply to can be so time-consuming, it may feel like once you get your documents in front of prospective employers, it's time to hand the reins to them. But even if you feel like you'd happily work for any of the organizations you've applied to, simply saying "I'm open" to lots of different opportunities may not work in your favor. Doing enough homework to understand how your personal preferences line up with the organization's culture and the job's content is key.

Heidi Moawad, M.D., author of *Careers Beyond Clinical Medicine*, notes that employers want to know that you're interested in them specifically.

If you're too flexible, she says, "you could end up ruling yourself out as a candidate for anything. You can come across as sort of aimless. It can be a red flag for a recruiter because it appears you don't really know what you're looking for, and that you might not be a good fit, even though you're hoping to make yourself seem like a great fit."

Moawad adds that whether you're looking for a clinical or non-clinical job, in most cases, you will have many employment options. Prospective employers know this—which makes it all the more important to them that you're sure what you want.

"Employers want to know that you've investigated their specific area, and that you're willing to stick around and become good at [the job]," she says.

Cindric agrees, and says she looks for evidence of specific reasons in a candidate's cover letter and CV. "Why, specifically, us? What is the attraction to Geisinger?" She adds that the more thought you've put into what you are looking for, and the more specific you can be about it, the better.

"I've always told residents and fellows that the interview is a two-way street," Mahan adds. "It's not just about the organization finding the right candidate, it's about the candidate finding the right organization. You should be asking as many questions as you need to ask" to determine whether the organization and the job match your goals and personality. Preparing good questions for the interview will help you evaluate the potential fit and reassure the recruiter you understand the job and the organization you're applying for, improving the odds you'll stay employed if hired.

Cindric notes that some candidates falter at the interview stage because they haven't prepared for interview questions they should have expected.

For example, if you've briefly addressed a gap in training or a history of short-term jobs in your CV or cover letter, that probably helped you get to the interview stage—when you'll likely be asked to confirm or elaborate on your explanations. And if you're leaving employment, you should be prepared to explain—clearly and without disparagement—why you're leaving that job.

"If they're talking negatively about their current employer, or about administration or their colleagues, that's a sour note," Cindric notes. "As a recruiter, I'm listening to learn whether they collaborate well."

"It's better not to be really critical of your current place [of employment] or previous place," Moawad adds. She also advises that candidates be prepared for recruiters to ask for references and have them ready, even if you intend not to provide them until an offer is pending.

"It's perfectly OK not to include references on your resume when you're applying," she says. But if you're asked for them and are concerned that your job search might get back to your current employer, 'Just say, 'Well, I would be happy to give you references, but I'm a little concerned about how this will come across in my current job.'"

Moawad suggests asking the recruiter how serious they are about your candidacy and explain that you would prefer to provide references only when and if the employer is preparing to make an offer. "It's very natural not to want everyone to know you're looking [for a new job]. Knowing that the reason you're not providing references right away isn't because [you're hiding] something bad, it's because you're concerned that your current employer doesn't know you're looking to leave, will reassure the recruiter."

Bungling the basics

Another red flag recruiters report seeing far too often: basic, avoidable errors in candidate CVs and cover letters.

One of the most important: missing information, including subspecialty qualifications, certification and licensing status, and visa requirements.

"We have credentialing requirements in which the physician needs to be board certified within a certain amount of time," Cindric says. "If I see a candidate that is still board eligible and they have been out of training for some time, that's a red flag to me. Now I'm wondering, did they take their boards and fail them? Or are they acquiring hours credited in order to be able to sit for their boards?" She adds that in some less-common cases, physicians who've been out of training for a while accumulating hours may qualify for grandfathering. Physicians in this situation should be sure to explain it in their CVs, to avoid confusion and hesitancy on the part of the recruiter.

Biga agrees that these details are critical—and notes that if a physician submits a CV that is missing board certification status, she's likely to reject it out of hand.

"If you're applying for an advanced heart failure position, and you're not boarded in heart failure yet but you're planning to sit for boards, explain that in your cover letter [or CV]. Don't make me ask," she says.

She also notes that in some cases, physicians seem to focus on filling their CVs with multiple pages of published papers, but organizations like hers are much less concerned with these publications than with the procedures a physician can perform. This is an example of how targeting the CV to your job goal is important— and why it's crucial to remember who your audience is.

"The papers are great if you're going to academia," Biga says, but much less relevant to a private-practice network like the one she leads.

For candidates who require visa sponsorship, Cindric notes, it's also essential to state that on their CVs, including the type of visa. This helps the recruiter know at a glance whether the physician is a feasible candidate for an open position. She adds that while Geisinger has immigration attorneys to help newly hired physicians work through visa issues, withholding visa requirements from the CV in hopes of negotiating a solution with the employer just wastes everyone's time.

"That's a bad idea," Cindric says. "If we can't sponsor, there's no further action we [or any employer] can take. It's not something we can navigate or negotiate, because it's guided by state and federal law."

While omitting key information is one big physician CV red flag, revealing unnecessary information on CVs and cover letters creates its own problems, since it may make a recruiter uncomfortable with circulating your documents.

"I've seen CVs with Social Security numbers, names of family members, and even blood types on them," Mahan says. She reminds candidates that "your CV is a professional document. It should focus on the professional. Just like in social media, you're putting this information out publicly."

While some sensitive information will be required if you're eventually hired, sharing it before you've been offered the job risks your private data being breached. "What if the recipient's email is hacked or you accidentally send your CV to the wrong person?" Mahan says.

Other issues that bug recruiters include typos, formatting problems, and other mistakes that suggest carelessness or lack of consideration.

Your cover letter and even your CV should always be customized for the opportunity, Mahan advises. "I've gotten cover letters addressed to the wrong company or a different person," she says. Taking the time to customize each submission gives you one more chance to catch such errors before you hit "send."

Typos might not be deal-breakers, especially if demand exceeds supply for the position you're interested in. But Biga says that when she sees CVs with bad typing, bad punctuation, bad layout, this sloppiness reflects poorly on candidates. She encourages all candidates to have someone they trust, such as their program director, take a close look at the document before they send it out to prospective employers. "Ask them, 'Is this somebody you would call?'"

Sometimes, Biga laments, CV problems can be even more basic. "Sometimes I look at a CV and say, 'You gotta be kidding me. No phone number.'" She reminds candidates that the CV should make it easy for the recipient to get in touch with you—via *their* preferred channel.

"I'm not going to email them. I'm not on Twitter. You need to give me your phone number because I'm going to text you." And, she adds, the phone number and email you provide should be your personal information—not your work contacts. Including a work phone number or email increases the likelihood that your "confidential" search could end up being accidentally revealed by a recruiter.

"Another thing recruiters look at is just the basic formatting of the CV. Is it scattered, are there different fonts? That conveys to me that they may not have taken [enough] time and may not be serious about their presentation," Cindric adds. To avoid this negative impression, she says, "be cognizant of a nice, clean format with consistency and good flow, so that when I as a recruiter look at it, the story makes sense." Saving all of your documents as PDFs also ensures that recipients see them as you intended them to look.

Shortening the CV when the opportunity doesn't require a complete bibliography is another way to be considerate of the reader. Moawad adds that even when prolific publishing is valued, such as when applying for academic and research-oriented jobs, too many pages can be unwieldy for the reader. Instead, she suggests spotlighting a few select publications and including a link to a complete list. "If you really want to show off how many you have, you can include a statement like 'over 50 publications' along with the link."

Cindric adds that a thank-you note is a very nice touch that many candidates overlook. Aside from conveying good manners, the note gives candidates another chance to reiterate and reinforce what they're looking for and how well they fit the job, she says.

Over-reliance on headhunters

Another potential red flag that physicians may be unaware of is depending too much on contingency recruiters—aka headhunters.

"If they're a strong candidate, I'll wonder why they're using an external recruiter," Biga says. Biga points out that it's usually easy to find in-house recruiters for any organization you're interested in. For example, you can get contacts through local chapters of your specialty society, networking with other physicians, or internet searches of practices and hospitals in the area. The cost of hiring through headhunters is always high, Biga adds—and the money she saves can be funneled back into hiring bonuses for applicants who contact her group directly.

Relying on contingency recruiters instead of researching and tracking down in-house recruiters directly may seem like an easy way to simplify your search, but you may miss out on some excellent physician job opportunities. What's more, even when some of the jobs or organizations you're targeting are handled primarily by headhunters, it's important to manage your own job search.

"It's up to you to take responsibility for this career transition," Moawad says. "The recruiter is not like your personal mentor or coach. You have to show that you're willing to meet them more than halfway."

If a recruiter feels that you're expecting they'll find a job for you—that you're putting the responsibility for your job search on their shoulders—that's a red flag. The recruiter won't just feel overburdened, Moawad notes. They may wonder if you're a strong or serious candidate they should recommend to their employer client.

"Remember that the recruiter doesn't want you to look bad," Moawad adds. "So show them you actually are going to do your part."

A shorter version of this chapter appeared as a feature in PracticeLink magazine's Summer 2022 issue.

CHAPTER 12: FROM REVENUE TO RVUS: DECODING PHYSICIAN PAY

Whether you're looking for your first post-training position or planning to change employers, odds are some of the job offers coming your way will include a productivity component. According to the Medical Group Management Association's (MGMA) 2019 compensation survey, nearly a third of primary care positions and more than 22 percent of specialist jobs include some portion of compensation determined by productivity.

Yet for many physicians, the prospect of tying a significant proportion of their pay to production is nerve-racking. Productivity compensation means uncertainty, and that leads some physicians to favor offers with straight-salary compensation only. But rejecting productivity-based compensation out of hand may be costly, especially over the long run. By limiting your search to positions offering straight salary, you may be closing yourself off from employers or locations you might prefer—and, quite possibly, more money.

"Some docs shy away from productivity incentive compensation because they're concerned about or don't understand it, but they're leaving money on the table," says Samuel Gerhardt, D.O., MBA, chief resident in family medicine at Methodist Hospital in Henderson, Kentucky. Gerhardt notes that, just like medicine,, business and compensation are specialized fields with their own terminology—concepts that physicians are rarely exposed to in medical school and residency. Then along comes an offer with a multi-faceted compensation plan, and "what usually happens is the physician sees the complex pay model and drops it because they don't understand it."

Gerhardt points out that physicians are, by their nature, accustomed to making decisions that rely on deep expertise. Productivity compensation schemes can play havoc with that expectation. "When you're in a situation where you're no longer the expert, you back off. When you only understand the base salary, that's the only thing you can look at."

Productivity compensation in context

Some physicians may also be concerned that measuring productivity takes the focus off patient care. Says Seger Morris, D.O., internal medicine program director and division chief, Mississippi internal medicine programs at Baptist Memorial HC in Oxford, Mississippi, "It very much is my experience that physicians are nervous about productivity, but I don't think they should be."

Morris asserts that modern medical training, in which residents are assigned fewer patients than in the past, may give new physicians a too-conservative sense of the workload they'll be able to handle. "Physicians coming out of training are not being trained in starting a business. They're being trained to be employed. Volume is completely deemphasized, even discouraged in most programs. Throughout your training, there is very little about what the real world will expect in terms of your productivity."

In some ways, Morris says, expectations about productivity that are set in training have changed more than actual physician practices have, whether in a hospital, large group, or private setting. Doctors are in short supply, and patients need care—and the same regulations that seem to deemphasize volume, including the ACA, also mandate that access to care be more universal.

Gerhardt agrees. "Some physicians get interested in MIPS—thinking that it [and other quality programs] will change everything. But improved quality won't replace the need for people who can see more patients. Speed and efficiency are still what makes money in any setting."

In the simplest terms, productivity-based compensation is pay based on the volume of work a physician does. There are multiple ways that volume can be calculated, and that complicates things a bit. But a well-designed productivity incentive program can be a much fairer arrangement for both the physicians and their employers than a one-salary-fits-all flat compensation arrangement.

"Some physicians are risk averse, and [prefer straight salary because they] just want to know what they'll be paid," says Satish Prabhu, M.D., owner and medical director of Rainbow Kids Clinic in Clarksville, Tennessee. "But their employers want to share risk."

Prabhu says that productivity-based compensation can be a win-win because it enables physicians to earn more pay by allowing their employers to manage business risk. Compensation that corresponds to production also helps reward clinicians who face unexpected increases in workload—for example, from an unusually stressful flu season or a colleague's maternity leave or retirement. This can head off resentments and bolster morale.

Productivity-based compensation can also provide physicians with much more flexibility, Prabhu adds. For example, he says, a physician could financially prepare to buy a home, pay down debt, or plan for an extended vacation by taking advantage of the option to earn by taking on more work.

How productivity compensation models work: the outlines

Compensation for employed physicians is typically structured as a mix of salary and incentives (i.e., bonuses). The salary is the guaranteed portion of a physician's earnings—what you might think of as the amount paid to you to show up for work and complete the basic requirements of your job. Incentive compensation is a means for your employer to recognize—and encourage—more value creation on your part. It's pay that's usually based on some measure of productivity, typically calculated based on billable services rendered or actual collections. It can make up a tiny percentage of compensation (even zero when straight salary is offered) or as much as 100 percent. (In 2018, the American Medical Association (AMA) reported that about 32 percent of physician compensation, on average, was driven by personal productivity.)

In hospitals, HMOs, and other large organizations, productivity is often calculated based on work RVUs (wRVUs), a standardized measure of physician effort assigned to each medical billing (CPT) code. Andrew Hajde, CMPE, assistant director of association content at MGMA, sees an ongoing trend of larger employers moving away from measuring productivity using revenue and toward an RVU-based approach. "Work RVUs are a fairer way to gauge work and effort," he says. He notes that since RVUs track the type of work performed and not revenues received, using RVUs frees employed physicians from worrying about how much a patient's health plan pays or how effective the billers are. Most electronic medical records systems also make it easy for physicians to track their own RVUs.

Revenue-based calculations of productivity are still preferred in many environments, though. And while RVUs create a standard productivity measure that doesn't vary based on how much is paid by a health plan, in some ways, revenue is a more familiar and straightforward metric for physicians.

"I cannot tell you how many students in our residency program don't understand an RVU or wRVU," Gerhardt says. "It's a mask hiding what they're going to get paid, when the employer could just say you're getting this percentage of collections minus overhead."

Revenue-based productivity helps encourage proper coding and documentation, too. Employers want to be sure physicians give these administrative tasks sufficient attention, since they're important determinants of how much and how quickly your employer will get paid.

Before your search: Empower yourself with information

Since a productivity compensation arrangement could be a part of any job package you're offered, arming yourself with a bit of knowledge can prepare you to understand the terms and negotiate.

Becoming familiar with common productivity benchmarks is a good first step. Many organizations use MGMA compensation and cost-survey data, for example, to set thresholds for productivity incentives. MGMA's Hajde points out that while access to complete MGMA survey data requires a subscription or membership, the association publishes select metrics each year via numerous channels, and it's possible to find some older data online. (Specialty societies often do their own surveys, too—and may make some reports available for free—or at low cost—for members.)

If you're not yet at ease with CPT coding, getting there before you start job searching in earnest is also helpful. Being able to bill with confidence will serve you well in your new job—and help you evaluate and make the most of productivity compensation.

Morris notes that CPT codes provide the RVU data that often determines productivity—so understanding CPT coding in your specialty will help you understand how your expected billing patterns will affect your income.

"Your specialty society and other medical organizations are good places to start," Morris says. He adds that for evaluation and management coding, E/M University can be a great resource. Without a solid understanding of CPT coding, he adds, you could "end up seeing more patients than necessary" to meet your RVU goal.

Researching supply and demand in the area where you plan to live can give you a feel for how hard it will be to build a practice. There are numerous databases online to help you calculate how many physicians in your specialty are practicing in your target location and compare those numbers with population trends. As Prabhu points out, it's much easier to build a high-productivity practice if the patient population is growing and new patients are looking for doctors.

Mike Blaney, general surgeon and founder of Live Healthy MD in Augusta, Georgia, adds that your employer's contracted insurers—aka, payer mix—may also make a difference in your earning potential. "In Beverly Hills, you'll find 80 percent or more of your patients will have good commercial insurance, with excellent reimbursement. But in other parts of the country, your practice might be as much as 50 percent Medicaid," he says.

Payer mix will have a direct impact on productivity pay that's tied to net collections—and, at the extremes, also affect how much your employer can afford to pay you in salary. Having a basic understanding of reimbursement economics can help you project the sort of offers you might get and where there could be room to negotiate more pay if you can deliver higher productivity.

Ask about key factors that enable productivity

Your own drive and initiative are essential to reaching volume targets, but it's unlikely you'll reach your highest productivity without the support of your employer. One of the first things you should explore in employment discussions is what sort of resources will be provided to help you get there.

You'll want to know, for example, if your employer plans to invest in marketing your new practice, as well as how much business development you'll be expected to do on your own.

For specialists, developing a network of referring primary-care physicians takes time. Will you be able to rely on overflow from the other physicians in the practice to fill your schedule while you make connections in the local community? Will you receive a higher salary while you build your stream of patients—and for how long?

"Some physicians have the personality to go and sing their own praises," says Blaney. "Others have more farmer than hunter mentality." It's important to know what the expectations around self-promotion are, and to think about ways to meet them that fit your personality. And if the practice expects you to build a flow of referrals from scratch, you'll need to know how long they expect that to take, and whether you'll receive a higher salary guarantee during that build-up period.

Primary care physicians should ask how many new patients are joining the practice each month and how they're assigned. If the local market is not growing, how does the practice plan to attract new patients for your panel? The type of patients likely makes a difference, too. For example, in an OB/GYN practice, having enough new patients of childbearing age can be important if maternity care is the fastest way to earn productivity compensation.

Prabhu suggests that pediatricians ask how newborns are assigned. Babies have many more check-ups per year than older children, so having more infant patients helps boost a pediatrician's numbers. Similarly, he adds, a pediatrician taking over for a retiring physician should ask about that doctor's patient demographics. If many of those patients are teenagers, they may soon leave a gap in the panel when they move on to an adult primary-care practice.

Physicians should also make sure they'll have enough support staff. Says Hajde, physicians should ask, "Will I be able to get an extra medical assistant if I'm a high performer? Will I get a scribe?"

Prabhu agrees. His practice was one of the first in Tennessee to be certified as a patient-centered medical home (PCMH). "We created our own workflow initiative to help our physicians achieve the standards of PCMH and enable them to focus on patient care." Prabhu says it's critical to determine whether the employer understands how appropriate support enables physician productivity—and reduces stress.

Scheduling is an important factor in productivity, too, he adds. Physicians should ask about the time slots available, and whether they'll have input into setting them.

If you have any doubts about the achievability of productivity numbers, don't hesitate to ask for details.

Says Morris, "A good recruiter should be able to show you the number of patients you need to see to break even, and how much you'll make if you see two or three more than that." Examples of how the practice's physicians meet their numbers, including their schedules and the staff support they have, should be made available to you if you ask.

Test assumptions and look for "gotchas"

Once you're comfortable with the basics of an offer, it's time to dig into the math. As you do, assumptions and unintended traps ("gotchas") that can cost you money may surface. It's important to test your assumptions and ask detailed questions so that you fully understand how you'd be paid if you accept a job.

In some settings and some specialties, some of your work may—by law—not be eligible for bonus pay. For example, hospitals can't provide you with an incentive to recommend procedures they profit from. If you take on a role as a cardiologist, for instance, your employment may require reading echocardiograms, but that work may need to be excluded from productivity calculations.

"Different settings have different rules," says Morris. "In a large group, where the machine is not owned by the group, those readings can count toward productivity. But if you're employed by the hospital, and the hospital owns the machine, they can't incentivize doctors to do that work."

Billing processes can determine what counts toward productivity, too. For example, surgeries or maternity care may be billed as a global package. If your job will include maternity check-ups or surgical assists or follow-ups, those activities may be excluded from your productivity calculations.

If you're an office-based physician and you're inheriting a panel, the practice's internal standards for determining whether a patient is active can also affect productivity. "Some practices may consider a patient who hasn't been seen in 18 months to be inactive, but others might not until it's been three years," Prabhu says. The definition of active versus dormant makes a big difference in how much demand an inherited panel will actually provide.

Prabhu also advises physicians to consider how special skills they bring to their new practice might affect their productivity. For example, if you're being wooed partly because of language skills, will that mean you'll be seeing more non-English-speaking patients? "This could mean you will have more Medicaid patients and longer appointments," he says. "That would mean lower reimbursement and fewer appointment slots each day." Likewise, physicians who've had success working with patients with ADHD or autism may be expected to see more of those patients, and for longer visits. If a panel includes a higher proportion of more complex patients, that can also mean more time per visit to manage them, and neither reimbursement nor RVUs may offset that fully.

If your productivity is calculated based on your practice's profitability, you'll also need to pay attention to how overhead is allocated. In a multi-specialty practice, the economics may even vary from physician to physician.

Blaney recalls that early in his career, he was bringing in much more revenue from cash-based bariatric surgeries than some colleagues whose patients were primarily on Medicare or Medicaid. Because the cost allocations were based on revenue, he was charged for more of the overhead than he was actually consuming.

"I was bringing in 70 percent of the revenue but was paid only 25 percent of it after overhead," he says. Luckily, he was able to work out a fairer arrangement with his practice. But if you are an employed physician, especially in a larger organization, it may not be possible to revise the terms after you start—so it's important to understand how overhead will work up front, when there's still time to negotiate.

Get help if you need it

For many physicians, understanding productivity arrangements gets into business territory—something they might have hoped to avoid by going into medicine. But you need to know enough "to make sure you're not getting taken advantage of," advises Morris.

When the terms start to get confusing, retreating toward a simpler, salary-only deal may seem safer, but you'll likely forgo income potential. Moreover, though it may seem like you won't have to worry about productivity if you find an employment arrangement that's salary-only, that's unlikely to be the case.

As Hajde explains, "In most cases, physicians do have to grow their business. If they don't do it, health systems may have to let them go. It's the reality of being a physician today—the same as any other business."

A better option is to get help from experts to fill in the gaps of what you don't yet understand, such as from a physician contract review consultant. Such expert help will likely cost no more than a few thousand dollars—a modest investment that could pay itself back hundreds or thousands of times over through your career.

Legal advice is indispensable, too. "Get a healthcare attorney—not just a regular business attorney, but a lawyer with experience with health-care and physician contracts—to review any contract you're considering signing," Morris says.

A shorter version of this chapter appeared as a feature in PracticeLink magazine's Fall 2020 issue, along with the brief glossary, questions to ask, and sample math to follow.

Compensation Terms to Know

Benchmark—a statistic used for comparing performance against a broader population. Benchmarks used for productivity calculations are usually based on survey data produced by groups such as the MGMA.

RVU—"RVU" stands for "relative value unit"—a standardized measure that aims to assign value to each billable medical procedure.

wRVUs—RVUs include a percentage value for physician work, practice overhead, and malpractice insurance. "Work RVUs," or wRVUs, refers to the physician work component of a service's RVU total.

Gross charges—the amount billed for services, based on the practice fee schedule. These charges are usually much higher than the payments expected based on insurance contracts. Rarely, productivity compensation may be based on gross billings.

Gross collections—the amount of revenue eventually realized from billing insurers and patients.

Net collections—gross collections less an allowance for overhead and direct expenses. Many productivity pay plans are based on net collections, especially in private groups.

Overhead—the practice expenses that must be covered by net collections, including facility, staff, etc. These expenses are typically allocated by physician and deducted from net collections before calculating a revenue-based productivity bonus. The overhead allocation may be done by direct calculation of individual expenses, divided equally among all physicians, or by a hybrid or weighted percentage approach.

Some Questions to Ask Employers about Productivity Pay

1. **Marketing**: Will marketing or advertising be done to help me build my practice? Will cost be spread across the entire business, or deducted from mine alone? If marketing attracts new patients, how are they assigned to physicians? Am I inheriting a panel from a retiring or departing doctor, or am I starting from scratch?

2. **Exclusions:** Are any procedures excluded from productivity calculations? How will non-productivity tasks be shared? How will I be compensated if I'm asked to take on responsibilities like serving on committees?

3. **Support:** How many support staff will I have? How will they be trained? If my productivity increases, can I get more help?

4. **Payments and reporting:** How often are production bonuses paid? If I take paid time off or a leave of absence, how will this affect my future earnings? Can I have on-demand access to productivity numbers? (If not, how often will I receive reports?)

5. **Benchmarks:** May I see a sample of the benchmarks you're using and how productivity is calculated in practice?

6. **Panel management**: At what point are patients who've not been seen for a while considered to have left the practice? If I inherit a panel with many inactive or aging patients, will I have assistance to reactivate them or expand my panel?

7. **Special skills:** What happens if my ability to handle special situations (e.g., non-English-speaking patients, patients with autism or dementia, etc.) affects the number of patients I can handle or expected revenue per patient? Will my productivity pay be adjusted for these time-consuming contributions?

8. **Compensation mix:** If I prefer to have a higher base salary and lower bonus potential, is this negotiable? If I participate in quality programs and help improve metrics, will I earn bonuses for this as well?

9. **Ramp-up time:** If I'll need to build my own panel, will I be paid a higher salary initially? Will I receive help with networking, such as introductions to hospital colleagues and staff, promotion to local primary care physicians, and reimbursement for joining networking groups and attending (or leading) events?

A Productivity Pay Example: How a Little Math Makes a Big Difference

Samuel Gerhardt, D.O., is both a practicing physician and a consultant who helps other physicians analyze their compensation options. Gerhardt has worked with colleagues who've been tempted to reject productivity-based plans out of hand—even when a little focused calculating is all that's required to make a better decision.

In particular, RVU programs can seem more complicated than they actually are, and that can lead to physicians choosing a "safer" option over a "riskier" bet that almost certainly will mean more income.

"It takes a little legwork to understand [productivity compensation], but it's worth it," he says. "It could make a big difference in your compensation over the next two to five years of your career."

Here's an example in which a physician is hypothetically offered two contracts*. Under option A, the physician would receive a salary of $240,000 and a bonus of $42 per wRVU for all wRVUs exceeding the $240,000 threshold. Option B has a $210,000 base salary with $50 per wRVU.

At first glance, option A seems the safer choice. The $240,000 in base salary, guaranteed, is significantly higher than option B. But is the first impression accurate?

In both cases, the base salary must first be earned out based on the same wRVUs that determine the bonus—a common approach. A little arithmetic reveals that the first option may not offer a clear income advantage at all.

Consider that:

- Under Option A, $240,000 base and $42/wRVU equates to 5,714 wRVUs per year before a bonus is earned.
- Under Option B, $210,000 base and $50/wRVU equates to 4,200 wRVUs per year before the bonus is earned.

This means that to surpass the guarantee and start earning bonuses, a physician must produce one-third more RVUs under Option A than under Option B.

More important: to earn $240,000 under Option B, the physician only needs to produce 4,800** RVUs—still about 20 percent less than Option A! And... all work performed beyond those 4,800 RVUs will earn $50/RVU (versus $42 under the "higher" plan).

Gerhardt also notes that these differences in RVUs translate to a big variance in workload.

Consider this calculation, based on outpatient-only family medicine data from MGMA, which shows the average patient visit generates 1.62 wRVUs:

- Under Option A, to reach $240,000 requires 5,714 wRVUs in a year, meaning 3,527 encounters (i.e., 5,714÷1.62).

- Under Option B, to reach $240,000 requires 4,800 wRVUs or 2,963 encounters (i.e., 4,800÷1.62)

Assuming a weekly schedule of 36 hours of clinic time and four hours of administration, plus four weeks of vacation and one week of CME, these two options differ greatly in daily workload.

Assuming about 1.2 RVUs per patient visit, Option A would require about 19 visits per day, while under Option B, the $240,000 threshold would require an average or 23 visits per day.

In this example, to lock in the higher guarantee under Option A, the physician is also committing to a plan that makes it very difficult for the physician to earn any more than the guaranteed base. Conversely, by accepting a little more risk, the physician can earn more with a less stressful schedule—and have much more upside if they work harder. While all the numbers here are hypothetical, the trading of a bit more risk for a shot at more income is the philosophy on which most productivity incentives are based.

Bottom line: It's worthwhile to sharpen your pencil and do this math when evaluating offers, because assumptions about salaries versus productivity pay can be misleading—and costly!

Example courtesy of Samuel Gerhardt, DO

**The numbers in this example are purely hypothetical. They're intended to illustrate the math only and should not be used as benchmarks to evaluate any actual offer received. But it's interesting to note that as of this writing, average primary care annual RVUs are estimated at 4,700-5,000 per full-time physician. In this hypothetical, this would put annual pay of more than $240,000 well within the reach of the average physician. Again, these hypothetical numbers shouldn't be relied upon, but they do illustrate the importance of knowing typical production levels for your specialty (and in the practice you're considering joining, too).*

CHAPTER 13: MID-CAREER PHYSICIANS SPEAK: WHAT I WISH I'D KNOWN IN RESIDENCY

As a job-seeking resident or fellow, you may feel multiple kinds of pressure. *Financial pressure. Peer pressure.* Perhaps above all, pressure to impress potential employers, so that you can accomplish this next step with the same high-achieving style that carried you from college through your medical training.

But the good news is, physicians who've gone before you—whether they're a few years out of training, nearing retirement, or somewhere in between—are happy to help. They've learned a thing or two since leaving residency, and they're glad to share what they wish they'd known when they were in your shoes. Here are seven of their lessons learned.

It's time to put yourself first—for the greater good

Kristin Miller, M.D., a family medicine physician with a hospital system in Oklahoma, says, "I didn't learn to advocate for myself in residency. I was always a people pleaser. I thought that was how you win in life. But I've learned it's actually the opposite. When you advocate for yourself and know what you need, and you're advocating for being the best version of yourself, that's how you win."

Now that hiring physicians is part of her job, Miller has a fuller appreciation of how important it is to be forthright during the interview process. "In residency, your goal is to get every single person to like you and want you. But in job hunting, you need to be choosy, and not just for yourself. It's only a win-win if you like them *and* they like you. This is a dynamic residents aren't used to."

Miller says fear of seeming impolite may lead residents to shy away from asking important questions during job interviews. But if physicians don't get the answers they need to make good decisions, they're likely to wind up in jobs that don't suit their goals or personalities. When unhappy physicians leave soon after they're hired, it's not just a loss for them. The costs to their employers can be substantial, both because recruiting is expensive and because physicians who exit within a year or two probably never reached a profitable level of productivity.

That's why savvy employers look for signs during interviews that candidates have done their homework, Miller adds. Smart, detailed candidate questions are an important indicator of interest and engagement. If you aren't prepared to ask meaningful questions, you may even limit your job opportunities.

"We don't want to hire people who don't ask questions," she says, noting that her hospital seeks evidence that candidates understand the work environment and culture and look forward to being a part of it. "We want people who are all in."

The right job might not be advertised

Oluwatoni Aluko, M.D., MPH, a family medicine physician in Philadelphia, says the power of networking to boost a physician's career wasn't emphasized during her residency. She found that out through experience, by not being shy about exploring her interests.

"You will get a lot of emails from recruiters," Aluko says, "[but] connecting with physicians first-hand gives you insight into what positions are available, many of which may not be advertised."

Aluko explains that during her residency at the University of Pennsylvania, she gained a fuller understanding of the clinical scope of student health clinicians during her rotations. She found herself drawn to that field and took the initiative to learn more about it.

"I reached out to an advisor to see if it was possible to create an elective in student health," she says. That contact led to a personalized elective and, not long after that, a job offer at Penn. "When I was ready to work and a position became available, the medical director and my colleagues in student health remembered me. [The elective rotation] was instrumental to me being top of mind when a position came open."

Now Aluko wants residents to know that investigating interests that are slightly outside the box can lead to opportunities that aren't part of the annual recruiting process—opportunities that might be a stronger match for your interests. Reaching out to meet physicians in less-publicized practice areas might not result in a job immediately, but Aluko stresses that this doesn't mean the effort is wasted. Making connections to physicians in fields you're interested in can put you in line for possibilities down the road.

"The worst they can say is there's nothing open. But at least you can ask. In the world of medicine, people talk. They remember you and refer you on."

Adrienne Youdim, M.D., FACP, a physician, author, and entrepreneur in Beverly Hills, also found herself on an atypical path during training and in the early years of her career. Diverging from her long-held plan created challenges, but what she discovered about her own goals and possibilities was invaluable. Now, she wants to pass on what she's learned.

"I matched in a very competitive [gastroenterology] fellowship when I got pregnant, and I decided I had to drop it," Youdim recalls. "But then I thought, what can I do now?"

The fellowship was a hard-won goal that arose from Youdim's interest in the technical side of medicine. Leaving it behind was difficult and left the way forward unclear, but also allowed Youdim to think more expansively about her options. When she learned about the surgical weight loss practice at Cedars-Sinai in Los Angeles, she decided to approach the medical center about creating a medical counterpart.

"I started up the Center for Medical Weight Loss at Cedars and ran it for ten years. We transitioned [the program at Cedars] from surgical weight loss only to both medical and surgical. We created a comprehensive program, and I became its co-director."

That experience gave Youdim the confidence and a platform to try other interests, like entrepreneurship and publishing. Since her time at Cedars, she has started her own practice, launched a nutrition line, and recently published a book, *Hungry for More*.

"I learned from patients that their desire for food is really a hunger for something else—and I thought about how that [process of introspection] applies to me as well. I learned that for me, the lack of autonomy in employed practice was not conducive to my goals. I had a lot of creative pursuits I was interested in."

Given the long on-ramp to becoming a physician, it's no small matter to contemplate a less predictable path while in residency or even the early post-training years. But Youdim will tell you it's been more than worth it for her. "There's so much benefit to giving yourself permission to evolve, to go where you need to. It doesn't mean you're not working hard. I am probably working harder now [than when I was employed]. But I have autonomy. I have purpose. I have creativity."

Conventional wisdom can be wrong

Looking back, some physicians also point out that job-related conventional wisdom you absorb in residency can simply be wrong—or, at least, wrong for you. There's no harm in questioning what "everyone says." Doing so might open the door to a job that's better for you.

"During training, you hear strong biases against certain practice types. Don't let others' views influence you. Independently evaluate each type—and each individual practice—for yourself," says Jay Wofford, M.D., FAAD, a dermatologist and dermatopathologist with US Dermatology Partners in Dallas, where he is also the group's North Texas regional president.

For example, negative views about private equity financing in medicine are common, but Wofford says the more he learned about US Dermatology Partners, a private equity-backed group, the more he believed their way of doing things fit his goals, which included dividing his time equally between a general dermatology practice and pathology work. It helped that US Dermatology Partners' lead marketer invested significant time on relationship-building with physicians in Wofford's residency. Wofford took advantage of the opportunity to meet with her, get answers to all his questions, and gain a clearer picture of what the group had to offer.

Chatter about private practice can also be dismissive in some residency programs, and colleagues may appreciate that hospital or health-system employment could allow them to focus on medicine (and not the management details of running a practice). But you owe it to yourself to explore private practice if you're curious about the added autonomy and business upside ownership may provide. What's more, with many specialties usually in high demand, you're unlikely to close the door on health system or hospital employment (or any other organization type) simply by trying out a private setting.

Wofford adds that for a clearer picture of what work life is like in any type of organization (or even specific practice), there's no better resource than physicians who currently work there. He urges residents to stay in touch with colleagues as they progress through residency. "Keep in touch with residents a year or two ahead of you who have similar interests. Find out how they started their search and narrowed it and get feedback from them as they start in the jobs. You can learn from their successes and mistakes." Wofford says that about six months after these colleagues start work is a good time to reach out to them. "Ask them if there's anything they wished they'd asked during interviews."

Learn what drives the business side—and your compensation

Elizabeth Chiang, M.D., Ph.D., an ophthalmologist and oculo-plastic specialist in Cleveland, found herself drawn to private practice, particularly the opportunity to hire her own staff and establish a more flexible work life. As she completed her training, she looked to join a private group on a partnership track and found multiple opportunities to consider. To decide where to land, though, she needed to learn what questions to ask.

Once Chiang homed in on a practice to join, she asked the owner for financial documents and enlisted her mother (a CPA) and her sister (a businesswoman) to help her confirm the business was financially sound. Chiang found much to like about that first job—but eventually she learned some important (but frustrating) lessons. "It was a good practice and well run. Support staff was great, and I had the flexibility I wanted. The problem was, I wasn't busy enough."

The practice owner had set a limited budget for marketing Chiang's new practice and wasn't willing to increase it when she asked. Although she was prepared to work hard to earn more, without more marketing support, her ability to grow her patient base was limited—a potential problem for any physician whose compensation depends on productivity.

Now Chiang advises job hunters to ask whether the job they've applied for is open because a physician is retiring or because the practice is growing. "If they say they're hiring because of growth, ask how fast the practice is growing and how they will support you with marketing," she says.

Wofford agrees that productivity (and income) are influenced by multiple factors outside a physician's control. He urges residents to learn about these levers and ask about them in interviews. For example, he says, your production may quickly hit a ceiling if you don't have enough staff support. Candidates should ask potential employers what productivity milestones determine when physicians can add a nurse or medical assistant.

"I wish I'd paid more attention to the practice management side of medicine," he says. "In residency, it's so easy to focus only on learning your specialty. That's obviously of the utmost importance. But once you get that underway, take a look at practice management. You need to understand it to make an educated choice."

When compensation is based on a percentage of collections, Wofford adds, "some residents get too focused on the percentage of collections they'll be paid. They're hung up on 35 or 40 or 45 percent, but that number doesn't mean anything [by itself]. The same percentage may be very different dollar amounts in two practices, even if they're next door to each other." To get a truer gauge of your upside potential, Wofford advises asking potential employers about their payer contracts and reimbursements.

"I wish I'd paid attention to billing and coding as a resident," Chiang adds. "I only started learning as a fellow how to code for surgery. Coding as a new attending was overwhelming. By then, it was so much to learn."

Chiang points out that residents (and even newly employed physicians) often underestimate the importance of doing billing-related tasks properly. She says she'd tell residents, "Talk to your attending to learn what is required to support billing at each level. This is what gets you those RVUs or collections. If [your documentation is] not right and you're audited, you might even have to pay back money."

Know your worth—and protect it

Knowing how much you can—and should—expect to be paid can be one of the most difficult and mysterious aspects of the job search. The information often isn't readily available and asking about it can feel awkward and inappropriate. Sometimes, though, online research can unearth compensation data for a related job to help you assess whether an offer you've received is in the ballpark, says Aluko. She's quick to add, though, that she's not shy about contacting people she knows who work at an organization she's interested in.

"I called someone once and just asked straight up, 'What's the pay?' People aren't always willing or allowed to disclose. But I try to ask as much as possible," says Aluko. "For many [physician] jobs, people can have a lot of negotiating power, especially in a field like family medicine. I've learned anecdotally from talking to [other] female providers, we don't always negotiate for ourselves. But you definitely have to know your worth. Each job makes a big difference in your trajectory and your salary later on down the line."

Miller agrees. "Especially when it comes to money, we get uncomfortable about advocating for ourselves. We've learned that religion, politics, and money are impolite to talk about. So maybe you don't want to lead out with it. But as interviews progress, you will get comfortable, and then you'll have an opportunity to ask." She adds that when you're in a group interview—such as on Zoom—you may not want to discuss these specifics in front of everyone. "You can wait until you're one on one with the recruiter, then you can be frank."

Professional negotiating help is also available. These consultants have access to survey data that's used to set productivity targets—data that can help you understand what you'll need to accomplish to meet your financial goals.

"It's a few thousand dollars [to hire a consultant]," Chiang says. "I think it's well worth spending. You will get much more back. I probably could have gotten a larger signing bonus if I'd hired one of them."

Chiang adds that even if your job offers guaranteed income, it's up to you to make sure your worth is appreciated once you're on the job. She recalls being intrigued by a recent physician podcast about "intrapreneurs"—basically, employees who innovate inside their organizations and take responsibility for improving them. She says physicians can take this approach to elevating their profiles and making their contributions apparent.

Nurture your financial freedom

After years and years of hard work with little or no income—and, probably, a lot of accumulated debt—it's not surprising that many residents want to upgrade their lifestyles. Buying a nice house soon after they land that first job is a common aspiration. The problem is, doing so adds another big responsibility to the list, and if you don't end up loving that first job, a mortgage can make you feel trapped.

"Chances are, your first job is not going to be where you'll stay long term. Don't buy your dream house right away," Chiang says. "If you want to live in a house, you can rent a house. Make sure you are really at the point you can be certain before buying."

Avoiding financial traps like paying down debt too slowly or living beyond one's means will also ensure you have the flexibility to modify your career if you choose to in the future.

Miller adds that she was able to earn a lot of money right away, but found it wasn't as satisfying as she'd hoped. "Four years ago, I was super successful. I was in the top 1 percent of female earners. It all looked great from the outside, but I wasn't happy. I thought, is this it? What is wrong with me?" With the help of a life coach, she gained clarity about what she really wanted from her physician career. This helped her reset her priorities and make positive changes to her work life.

Don't postpone happiness

Miller's experience with coaching may reflect a promising new trend among physicians. She says that when she told colleagues about her experience, so many asked her to coach them that she trained up to become a coach for physicians herself—as did Chiang.

"I want to focus on helping doctors not feel like they're on the hamster wheel," Chiang says.

Chiang describes a self-defeating phenomenon she observed starting in residency: physicians putting off enjoyment of their careers and lives. "You go through residency thinking 'it'll be better when I'm a fellow.' Then in fellowship, you think, 'it'll be better when I graduate.' What I've learned is that it doesn't have to be about waiting until the next stage—it's about what you create. The mindset piece I learned in coaching taught me it's not just about getting things done. It's about how you feel in the process."

Ironically, forced time off during COVID opened the door to a new outlook for Chiang. "In a way, COVID had so many great things for me. Because we shut down for a while, I only worked one to two days per week. And things were happening online that hadn't been online before. I went to a free conference about physicians leveraging their experience and doing more than just being a physician. I heard about physicians doing real estate and venture capital, being expert witnesses, physicians who are life coaches. It was eye opening. I was in a place where I could interact with doctors doing all these amazing things besides just being a doctor."

One course Chiang took explored real estate investing as a path to financial independence and early retirement. Applying what she learned, Chiang now owns two investment properties and divides her time between practicing medicine and her business pursuits. This change helps her continue to enjoy her medical career and avoid burning out.

"There are a lot of simple practices that we ignore—not only physicians, but all of us—that truly enhance our wellbeing," adds Youdim. "Practices like movement, nutritive, wholesome food, sleep. More globally, a meditative activity can help you be intuitive about the direction your life will take, to let your true intentions guide you. Learning integrative techniques like mindfulness will not only improve your patients' care... it allows you to have a fulfilling career with greater meaning."

While successful medical professionals have internalized a culture of striving, Youdim observes, healing requires both intellect and humanity. "We can't let the first interfere with the latter. Competition and perfectionism can be counter to what we *do* and *are* as humans and can lead to not showing up as your best self, and to burning out."

Boundaries and balance are also key to a satisfying, sustainable career, says Aluko. "In a field like family medicine, patients are constantly in contact. Sometimes we get calls from patients we haven't even seen before." Aluko adds that patients aren't just calling, they're messaging physicians via patient portals as well. To manage the load, too many physicians wind up putting off important tasks like charting or taking work home with them—risking overwork and burnout. "Do today's work today. Rather than letting things pile up, be strategic about getting things done," Aluko advises. "I ask myself, what can I delegate?"

Aluko also wants the physicians coming up behind her to know that the long journey to a physician career is worth it—and that you should take advantage of all it has to offer.

"Residency can be really tough," she says. "It can feel like it will never end, but it will—and after it does, you get the flexibility to think about what you really want to do. Your first job doesn't have to be your forever job. Your first couple of years post residency are a time to get to know yourself and your interests, and to really hone your skills as a physician."

Above all, Aluko adds, your physician training is an asset no one can ever take away from you. "You'll always have the opportunity to pivot into new roles. If you decide you want to do medicine one day a week and also write a travel blog, that's a choice you're free to make. Life is too short to be miserable. You only have one life. Do what you love."

A shorter version of this chapter appeared as a feature in PracticeLink magazine's Winter 2022 issue.

FOOTNOTES

CHAPTER 1: MISTAKES JOB-HUNTING PHYSICIANS MAKE—AND HOW TO AVOID THEM

1. If a "recruiter" asks you to pay a fee, that's a red flag. A legitimate physician recruiter will not ask you for payment. Recruiters are hired by employers, not candidates. (This is different from, say, an expert compensation consultant you might hire to help you evaluate an offer.)

CHAPTER 2: MORE MISTAKES JOB-HUNTING PHYSICIANS MAKE—AND HOW TO AVOID THEM

1. Disability coverage is a complex topic that you should research carefully and explore thoroughly with an expert on physician plans.
2. As shown in studies like the MGMA Stat report from May 25, 2022.
3. This is a bit of an oversimplification. You can imagine a situation in which unexpected major expenses or revenue shortfalls in, say, another part of the hospital could be so severe that paying out bonuses to physicians who hit their highest productivity goals might still make a negative profit situation worse. But the idea is that by emphasizing productivity pay throughout an organization, that risk is reduced (especially in comparison to simply guaranteeing salaries with no differential for individual physician revenues).
4. As of this writing, the FTC is proposing to ban non-compete agreements altogether, at least for for-profit businesses. But the rule has some hurdles to clear before it can take effect.
5. Can you guess why I've put this in all caps? As a consultant, I've seen it too many times: contracts that were lost after years of house moves or just… life. Find a safe place for them so you'll always know where they are. (And if you start a practice of your own or become a partner of an existing one, this is a very important thing to do with your payer contracts, leases, and other critical documents, too.)

CHAPTER 7: SIMPLE STEPS TO A SUCCESSFUL COVER LETTER

1. Note that the examples are written by a non-doctor (i.e., me) and may not sound realistic or accurate to your ears. The point is just to get you thinking about the kinds of things you can include to give your letters interest and life.

ABOUT THE AUTHOR

LAURIE MORGAN is a medical practice management consultant, author, freelance journalist, and speaker. She has an MBA from Stanford University and a degree in economics from Brown University.

Laurie would love to hear from you! Contact her via her website (capko.com) or email (lmorgan@capko.com).

ALSO BY LAURIE MORGAN, MBA

People, Technology, Profit: Practical Ideas for a Happier, Healthier Practice Business

* 9 7 8 1 9 7 0 0 4 4 2 1 8 *